Trauma-Spending

Trauma-Spending

Matthew Petchinsky

1

Trauma-Spending: When Money Becomes a Drug

By: Matthew Petchinsky

Disclaimer

Trauma-Spending: When Money Becomes a Drug is a creative, educational, and motivational resource designed to explore the emotional, psychological, and behavioral patterns surrounding money addiction, impulse purchasing, financial self-soothing, and trauma-linked spending cycles. While this book discusses themes such as money addiction, compulsive buying, emotional spending, survival-mode behaviors, scarcity wounds, financial trauma, and nervous-system responses to stress, it is **not** written by a licensed therapist, psychologist, psychiatrist, financial advisor, addiction specialist, or clinical counselor.

All information presented within these pages is based on personal experience, research, observation, and transformative self-help methodology. The content is intended for **informational and reflective purposes only** and should not be interpreted as medical, psychological, psychiatric, or financial advice. Nothing in this book constitutes a diagnosis, treatment plan, therapeutic intervention, or professional recommendation regarding addiction, trauma, mental health, or financial decision-making.

If you are currently struggling with compulsive spending, financial addiction, severe emotional distress, untreated trauma, suicidal thoughts, or symptoms that disrupt daily functioning, it is strongly recommended that you seek qualified professional support. This may include—but is not limited to—licensed therapists, trauma-informed counselors, addiction specialists, certified financial therapists, psychologists, psychiatrists, or other professionals equipped to provide individualized care.

Readers are encouraged to make financial decisions with caution and personal responsibility. Strategies, exercises, reflections, and practices provided in this book should be adapted to your own circumstances and should never override advice from qualified professionals familiar with your situation.

By choosing to read this book, you acknowledge that you are fully responsible for your emotional and financial choices, and you agree that the author and publisher are not liable for any outcomes resulting from the application or misinterpretation of the material presented. This book is a supportive companion on your healing journey—not a substitute for therapeutic intervention, mental-health treatment, addiction counseling, financial planning, or crisis assistance.

If you are in immediate danger or experiencing a mental-health crisis, please contact emergency services or a crisis hotline in your area right away.

Introduction

When Money Becomes a Soothing Mechanism

From food to shoes to gadgets, trauma shopping doesn't always look dramatic. Sometimes it's the quiet click of "Add to Cart" after a hard conversation. Sometimes it's a late-night online order that promises comfort, belonging, or a momentary escape. Sometimes it's a brand-new outfit purchased not out of want, but out of the desperate hope that a new version of you will feel less broken than the old one.

Emotional spending is often misunderstood. To the outside world it may look like greed, irresponsibility, or carelessness. But for many people, compulsive buying is not about excess — it's about **pain relief**. It's about calming a nervous system that has been in survival mode for years. It's about distracting yourself from abandonment wounds, shame, loneliness, or the ache of feeling unseen. It's about using money the same way others use substances, relationships, food, work, or screens: **as a temporary escape from emotional pain you were never taught how to manage**.

This book begins with a simple truth:

Your peace cannot be purchased — but your healing can be reclaimed.

Trauma-spending is often rooted in experiences far older and deeper than the purchases themselves. Childhood scarcity. Emotional neglect. Living with chaos or instability. Surviving environments where safety was unpredictable or withheld. Growing up with the belief that having something new meant you mattered — even for a moment. Or that buying something small could give you a sense of control in a life that rarely offered any.

Over time, this pattern creates a cycle that feels impossible to break:

Trigger → Emotional overwhelm → Spending for numbness → Shame → Repression → Repeating the cycle.

This cycle doesn't make you weak. It makes you human.

In this book, we will explore:

- How trauma reshapes the brain's relationship with money.
- Why spending can mimic the neurological response of addictive substances.
- The science behind emotional regulation, dopamine spikes, and soothing behaviors.
- How childhood conditioning, instability, and unmet emotional needs shape adult spending patterns.
- The hidden cost of shame — and why self-blame keeps the cycle alive.
- How to gently untangle your identity from your purchasing habits.
- How to rebuild safety, self-worth, and emotional regulation without using money as a numbing tool.

But most importantly, this book will give you **compassion**, not judgment.

Because judgment never heals addiction — compassion does.

You will learn practical tools, trauma-informed strategies, and reflection practices to help you reclaim the parts of yourself that felt safest when spending. You'll understand the emotional script behind your triggers and discover healthier ways to soothe the wounds money has been covering for far too long.

This is not a book about shaming you into budgeting harder or depriving yourself. It is not a book about financial perfectionism or punishing discipline. Instead, it is a book about **healing the nervous system that keeps reaching for relief**.

Emotional spending may have been your lifeline.

It may have been your comfort.

It may have been your armor.

But it does not have to be your identity.

Your healing begins here — with understanding, with gentleness, and with the courage to stop buying peace and start building it instead.

Let's break the cycle with compassion, not condemnation.
Let's walk into a future where your worth isn't tied to what you buy, but who you become.

Chapter 1: What Is Trauma-Spending?

Trauma-Spending as a Survival Response, Not a Money Problem

Trauma-spending is not rooted in irresponsibility, greed, or poor financial discipline. It is rooted in the brain's attempt to regulate overwhelming emotions when traditional support systems are missing or unsafe. When the nervous system has been conditioned through pain, chaos, or instability, it begins searching for anything that resembles predictability or relief. Purchases—no matter how small—become a momentary anchor in a storm the body never fully escaped. Trauma-spending is the brain trying to create safety through action, not luxury.

When trauma has shaped a person's early environment, the brain becomes hyper-attuned to threats and discomfort. This state, known as chronic hypervigilance, depletes emotional resources. When the body learns that soothing never comes from people, environment, or support, it begins generating its own coping tools. For some, this becomes overeating or isolation. For others, it manifests in high productivity or people-pleasing. For many, it becomes purchasing. Spending becomes a self-initiated release valve—something you can control when the rest of life feels uncontrollable.

Over time, the brain begins associating buying with relief. It doesn't matter what is purchased; it matters that the act signals "momentary safety." Money becomes the medium through which reassurance is delivered. Trauma-spending, therefore, is not a financial issue—it is a nervous-system strategy. The body is not craving an object; it is craving stability, certainty, and peace.

Understanding this shift is the foundation of healing. You cannot shame yourself out of trauma responses. You cannot budget your way out of a nervous system stuck in survival mode. You heal this pattern not through punishment but through recognition: **you aren't broken—you adapted.**

How Trauma Reshapes the Brain's Relationship With Money

Trauma reshapes neural pathways, especially those involving safety, reward, and decision-making. When a child grows up in environments where money was scarce, unstable, unpredictable, or weaponized, the brain encodes powerful survival meanings onto finances. Money becomes more than currency—it becomes a symbol of safety, escape, comfort, or proof of worthiness. These emotional associations follow us into adulthood, silently interacting with every financial decision we make.

A traumatized brain tends to operate from the limbic system, the emotional center, rather than the prefrontal cortex, which regulates logic and long-term planning. This means that purchases often arise from emotional overwhelm rather than conscious intent. Trauma-spending happens when the brain's emotional center tries to override discomfort faster than the thinking brain can intervene. It is a reflex, not a choice.

The relationship between trauma and money becomes cyclical. The person feels stress → the body seeks relief → the brain recalls that buying triggered relief before → the cycle repeats. This can occur whether the person grew up poor, financially unstable, financially controlled, or financially overindulged. Trauma is not defined by circumstance; it is defined by emotional impact. And if money was ever tied to fear, deprivation, shame, or unpredictability, the brain develops patterns around it that persist for decades.

By understanding this, we begin unlocking the compassion needed to heal. Trauma-spending was never about carelessness. It was about survival. It was the best tool your younger self had at the time—and acknowledging that truth marks the beginning of liberation.

Why Spending Can Mimic the Neurological Response of Addictive Substances

Shopping activates dopamine, the brain's reward chemical. For people with trauma histories, dopamine often becomes the primary source of emotional regulation because nurturing, soothing, and safety were inconsistent or absent. When you buy something, dopamine spikes, cortisol lowers, and the nervous system experiences a temporary sense of relief. This is the same biological pattern seen in behavioral addictions such as gambling, binge eating, or compulsive social media scrolling.

Trauma survivors often have altered dopamine receptors due to chronic stress. This means everyday joys produce less stimulation, while soothing behaviors like shopping hit the brain harder. The purchase doesn't create joy—it creates numbness. It replaces emotional pain with a chemical distraction. The brain learns that spending "works," and once that association is formed, it reinforces itself automatically.

This neurological loop can continue even when the person logically knows that buying will lead to regret. Addiction is not defined by lack of intelligence; it's defined by the nervous system overriding logic to avoid emotional discomfort. Trauma-spending behaves like a chemical addiction because the brain is using dopamine as anesthesia. The object purchased is irrelevant—the dopamine spike is what matters.

Understanding this helps remove guilt. You never "lacked discipline." You lacked safer soothing tools. And this book is here to give you the tools you were never taught.

Childhood Roots: How Early Instability Shapes Adult Spending Patterns

Childhood experiences form the emotional blueprint for adulthood. When a child grows up in an unstable home—financially, emotionally, or physically—the brain wires itself to survive unpredictability. If resources were scarce, the adult brain may panic even when money is available. If love was withheld, the adult may buy things to feel worthy or lovable. If chaos was constant, spending becomes a ritual of predictability—one of the few things you could always control.

Children who grow up in financially unstable environments often develop "hyper-earning fantasies," believing money will finally create safety. Others develop "emergency spending patterns," fearing that if they don't enjoy something now, everything will be taken away later. For children who experienced emotional neglect, purchases become symbolic: "This new thing will make me feel better in ways people couldn't."

These patterns persist because trauma is not just memory—it is programming. The nervous system is conditioned by repetition. If chaos was repeated, chaos feels familiar. If scarcity was repeated, scarcity feels inevitable. If shame was repeated, shame becomes self-directed after purchases.

By identifying these childhood patterns, you begin dismantling their power. What feels like "just how I am" is often "just how I learned to survive."

Money as a False Safety Cue and Why You Aren't Broken

Money becomes a "false safety cue" when the brain interprets spending as protection from emotional danger. The temporary relief feels like safety—even when it isn't. Trauma survivors often feel unsafe in their bodies and environments, so they search for external anchors. Purchases become these anchors: something new, something stimulating, something controllable.

But purchases are temporary. They soothe symptoms, not causes. When the dopamine fades, the unresolved emotional wounds rise again, often triggering shame. This shame deepens the sense of brokenness, feeding the cycle further. But the truth is simple: you are not broken. You adapted to circumstances no one should have had to survive. Your brain preserved you using the tools available at the time.

Healing trauma-spending requires rewiring this safety cue. Instead of spending to regulate your nervous system, you begin regulating your nervous system so spending doesn't control you. This is not a quick fix—it is a reparenting process. It is emotional rehabilitation. And it is fully possible.

Self-compassion is the cornerstone of transformation. Without it, the nervous system stays in shame, and shame keeps the cycle alive. With compassion, the nervous system calms, logic returns, and healing begins.

Laying the Foundation for Compassionate Healing

Healing trauma-spending begins with permission: permission to forgive yourself, permission to understand your patterns, and permission to heal without punishment. Shame cannot create transformation; it only deepens emotional wounds and intensifies spending impulses. Compassion is the medicine your nervous system has been waiting for.

In this chapter, you are not asked to fix anything—only to understand it. Understanding is regulation. When the brain finally has a story for why it does what it does, it stops panicking. The subconscious softens. The survival urgency quiets. This shift is the beginning of recovery.

Compassion-based financial healing is not about strict budgets or deprivation. It is about slowly teaching the brain that safety exists in places other than purchases. It is about rebuilding trust with yourself—trust that you can feel discomfort without self-destruction. Trust that emotional pain no longer requires a financial anesthetic.

By approaching your spending history with tenderness rather than judgment, you begin creating the emotional stability necessary to stop trauma-spending at its root. You are not here to punish yourself. You are here to reclaim the parts of you that never got the safety they deserved.

20 Lessons for Understanding Trauma-Spending

1. Your spending habits formed as survival responses, not flaws.
2. Trauma changes how the brain interprets money and control.
3. Spending often mimics the relief response of addictive substances.
4. Dopamine spikes temporarily numb emotional pain.
5. Childhood scarcity imprints urgency onto financial decisions.
6. Emotional neglect shapes adult self-soothing behaviors.
7. Purchases become symbols when real comfort was unavailable.
8. Shame reinforces the cycle, not responsibility.
9. Trauma-spending begins long before adulthood.
10. The brain treats spending as predictable relief.
11. The thinking brain rarely participates in trauma-spending episodes.
12. The emotional brain is trying to protect you.
13. Healing requires nervous system regulation, not budgeting alone.
14. You cannot shame yourself into sustainable change.
15. Self-compassion repairs what shame destroys.
16. Safety must be rebuilt from the inside out.
17. Trauma-spending ends when emotional needs are met elsewhere.
18. You do not need to earn healing—you deserve it.
19. Emotional pain is valid, even if it expresses through spending.
20. You adapted to survive—and now you can adapt to heal.

The Safety Reset Ritual

Purpose: To retrain the nervous system to experience safety without spending

Time Required: 7 minutes

Tools: A chair, a pen, your hand resting over your heart

Step 1 — Anchor the Body

Sit in a steady chair. Place your feet flat on the floor. Rest one hand over your heart and one hand over your stomach. Breathe slowly for three cycles, letting your exhale be longer than your inhale. Tell your nervous system: "You are safe in this moment."

Step 2 — Identify the Emotional Trigger

Whisper aloud the emotion underneath your spending urge:

- "I am anxious."
- "I am lonely."
- "I feel rejected."
- "I feel overwhelmed."

Naming the emotion decreases limbic activity by up to 30%.

Step 3 — Replace the Cue

Say out loud: "Safety comes from within me, not from purchases."
Tap gently on your sternum twice. Feel the vibration.

Step 4 — Release the Urge Through Breath

Inhale through your nose for 4 counts, hold for 2, exhale for 6.
Repeat 3 times.

Step 5 — Seal the Ritual

Place your hand back on your heart and end with:
"I choose compassion. My body is learning safety again."

This ritual rewires your nervous system to reduce trauma-spending impulses over time.

Emotional Budgeting: The Feelings-First Financial Pause Method

1. **Pause:** Before buying anything, pause for 20 seconds.
2. **Locate:** Identify the emotion driving the impulse.
3. **Name:** Say the emotion out loud or write it down.
4. **Respond:** Choose one healthy emotional regulation tool (breathing, grounding, movement, journaling).
5. **Reassess:** Decide if the purchase is a need or a numbing tool.
6. **Proceed:** Move forward with intention, not impulse.

This method replaces financial shame with emotional clarity.

Three Trauma-Healing Exercises

Exercise 1: The Childhood Money Memory Map

Write three childhood memories involving money—positive or negative.
Next, identify the feeling in each memory.
Finally, write how those feelings show up in your current spending.
This draws a direct link between past and present.

Exercise 2: Emotional State Check-In Chart

Create three columns:

- What I Felt
- What Triggered It
- What I Wanted the Purchase to Fix

Filling this chart in after a spending impulse exposes patterns over time.

Exercise 3: The Somatic Urge Release

When you feel the urge to buy:

- Shake your hands for 10 seconds
- Roll your shoulders for 10 seconds
- Exhale with sound

This releases the stored energy that usually turns into spending.

Meditation: Sitting With the Urge Without Judgment

Close your eyes and breathe deeply. Visualize the spending urge as a wave rising in your body—not harmful, not dangerous, simply energy. Feel the wave peak, then imagine it slowly lowering. Tell yourself: "This feeling is temporary. I am safe even when uncomfortable." Allow the wave to pass without acting on it. End by placing your hand on your heart and saying: "I am learning a new way."

Ten Journal Prompts

1. What did money mean in my childhood?
2. When did I first use spending as comfort?
3. What emotions trigger my strongest spending urges?
4. What am I hoping the purchase will give me?
5. What does "safety" feel like in my body?
6. What financial patterns repeat across my life?
7. What am I afraid will happen if I stop trauma-spending?
8. How has spending tried to protect me?
9. What would emotional safety look like without buying anything?
10. What kind of relationship do I want with money in the future?

Closing Reflection

Trauma-spending is not a failure of discipline; it is a history of survival written into your nervous system. Every purchase you made to soothe pain was an attempt to feel safe, valued, or in control. This chapter is the beginning of rewriting that story. You are not here to punish your past self—you are here to understand them. With compassion as your guide, you will learn to meet your emotional needs without sacrificing your financial peace. Healing begins when shame ends—and today marks that shift.

Chapter 2: Shopping as Self-Soothing

Why We Shop to Soothe: Understanding the Emotional Landscape

Shopping draws in its power from emotional overwhelm, not desire. When a person feels anxious, lonely, ashamed, or abandoned, the nervous system sends distress signals demanding relief. In these moments, the body is not looking for logic—it is looking for safety. The act of buying feels like a temporary escape from the emotional chaos underneath. Trauma survivors often use shopping not to "treat themselves," but to treat their pain.

Behind every shopping impulse lies a sensation that feels too heavy to face alone. A person might be overwhelmed by responsibilities, grief, emotional neglect, or conflict. The spending impulse becomes a way to interrupt that discomfort. It temporarily shifts the emotional state, replacing chaos with a moment of predictable reward. Trauma survivors seek predictability above all else, and purchases—unlike people—do exactly what they promise: they arrive, they distract, they comfort.

For some, shopping fills the emotional gaps left by childhood experiences of neglect or instability. When someone grows up without consistent nurturing, objects can feel safer than humans. A new item becomes a symbol of care, even if the care comes from oneself. This symbolic self-parenting becomes woven into emotional responses, creating a soothing pattern as automatic as breathing.

Shopping is not a sign of weakness. It is a coping mechanism chosen by a nervous system that learned to survive without secure emotional support. And like any coping mechanism, its purpose is protection—not pleasure. Understanding this truth opens the door to compassionate healing.

The Neuroscience of Self-Soothing: How the Brain Uses Spending to Regulate Emotions

The brain's reward system is designed to keep us alive, and when emotional pain feels intolerable, it will reach for anything that promises relief. Purchasing triggers dopamine, the neurotransmitter that signals comfort, reward, and anticipation. In trauma-surviving brains—where dopamine pathways may be dysregulated—this hit feels especially relieving. The brain interprets this spike as safety, creating a loop that reinforces spending as the fastest form of emotional regulation.

When someone feels anxious, cortisol rises. Shopping temporarily reduces cortisol, lowering stress and creating calm. The body experiences a moment of relief, even if artificial. This relief becomes conditioned. Trauma survivors learn that spending is a reliable, fast-acting emotional stabilizer—unlike conversations, relationships, or environment, which may have historically felt unsafe or unpredictable.

The brain's logic center, the prefrontal cortex, often shuts down during emotional distress. This makes trauma-spending impulsive, automatic, and deeply tied to survival instincts. The purchase does not represent frivolity—it represents an attempt to regain emotional control. The brain is not saying, "I want something new." It is saying, "I need to feel okay."

Understanding these neurological responses removes moral judgment. Trauma-spending is not a character flaw—it is the brain doing its best with the tools it has. Rewiring this pattern begins with recognizing the biology behind it.

Self-Soothing Through Spending in Real Time: What It Looks Like Inside the Body and Mind

A trauma-spending episode often begins long before the moment a finger presses "Buy Now." It starts with an internal trigger: a conflict, a stressful memory, a lonely night, a difficult conversation, or a wave of anxiety. The body becomes dysregulated, and discomfort spreads through the chest, the stomach, or the shoulders. The mind begins scanning for something to interrupt the discomfort, and shopping appears as the fastest relief.

As the urge grows, the world narrows into a tunnel. The mind fixates on the idea of purchasing, imagining the comfort the object will bring. The heart rate increases, thoughts swirl, and the nervous system becomes flooded. The act of browsing becomes soothing itself—a momentary escape from emotional pain. People often mistake browsing for intentional shopping, but in reality, browsing is part of the regulation ritual.

Once a purchase is made, the dopamine surge creates instant relief. The moment feels like calm, control, and clarity. The nervous system interprets this as success: discomfort reduced, emotional pain numbed. The brain then reinforces the behavior by filing it under "effective coping mechanisms." With repetition, the connection becomes automatic: discomfort → browse → buy → relief.

But after the relief fades, the emotional pain often returns, accompanied by guilt or shame. This shame then becomes the trigger for another cycle. Understanding this sequence helps you see that trauma-spending is not random—it is a self-soothing ritual the nervous system learned for survival.

False Safety: How Shopping Gives Temporary Control While Deepening Emotional Wounds

Shopping creates an illusion of stability. When your emotions feel too big and life feels unpredictable, purchasing gives the false sensation of mastery. "I can choose something. I can control something. I can make myself feel better." Trauma survivors often lacked environments where emotional needs were met with love or security, making the feeling of control addictive.

Temporary control does not equal true safety. While the purchase provides relief, it does not resolve the root emotions beneath the impulse. The original pain remains stored in the body. Over time, spending becomes a displacement strategy: the emotional pain is transferred to a financial problem. But the wound itself remains unaddressed.

This false safety can mask deeper issues such as abandonment trauma, rejection trauma, emotional neglect, or chronic overwhelm. When the nervous system has not learned safe emotional processing, it tries to create artificial safety through external actions. Spending becomes a shortcut to serenity, but the serenity is momentary.

Replacing false safety with authentic safety requires compassion, somatic awareness, and emotional tools—not self-criticism. The goal is not to remove the need for soothing but to give the nervous system healthier methods of achieving it.

Creating Safe Alternatives: Introducing Healthier Soothing Without Shame

Healing trauma-spending does not begin by taking away shopping. It begins by introducing new ways to soothe your nervous system. Replacing spending with healthier regulation tools should feel supportive, not restrictive. Trauma survivors cannot heal by deprivation. They heal by increasing safety in small, repeatable ways.

Healthy alternatives work best when they address the specific emotion beneath the impulse. If the urge is triggered by anxiety, grounding techniques may help. If triggered by loneliness, connection-based tools may help. If triggered by overwhelm, sensory regulation may help. Healing requires understanding the emotional need first, then matching it with an appropriate soothing tool.

Sustainable healing also requires emotional permission. You must allow yourself to soothe without spending and without shame. Shame will only drive you back into the cycle. You are learning—not failing. Every attempt to soothe in a new way strengthens the neural pathway away from compulsive spending.

Introducing alternatives with compassion marks the beginning of emotional independence. You are teaching your nervous system: "You can feel, and you can survive the feeling."

Trauma-Informed Regulation Tools That Replace the Shopping Urge

Trauma-informed soothing tools work because they regulate the nervous system—not because they distract from distress. These tools reduce emotional flooding, restore connection to the body, and build tolerance for uncomfortable feelings. When practiced consistently, they rewire the need for shopping as the primary coping mechanism.

These tools help shift the body from survival mode into self-regulation mode. By stabilizing the nervous system first, you regain access to logical decision-making. This is how trauma-healing intersects with financial healing: emotional stability improves money choices.

Each tool is chosen for its ability to calm the limbic system (the survival brain) while strengthening the prefrontal cortex (the decision-making brain). Unlike deprivation-based strategies, trauma-informed tools soothe without shame, punishment, or pressure.

Over time, these tools help rewrite emotional scripts and break the cycle of trauma-spending. They teach the body that comfort is possible—even without buying anything.

20 Lessons

1. Shopping is emotional self-regulation, not indulgence.
2. The spending impulse begins long before the purchase.
3. Trauma survivors rely on fast, predictable relief.
4. Dopamine spikes feel like safety.
5. Emotional overwhelm triggers browsing behaviors.
6. The body seeks soothing, not objects.
7. Control feels intoxicating when the inner world feels chaotic.
8. Browsing is part of the regulation ritual.
9. Relief is temporary, not transformative.
10. Emotional triggers create financial behaviors.
11. Shopping cannot heal abandonment wounds.
12. Numbing is not the same as comfort.
13. Shame deepens the cycle, not discipline.
14. Regulation tools retrain emotional responses.
15. Healthier coping mechanisms create lasting safety.
16. Spending is the body asking for comfort in the only way it knows.
17. Self-awareness interrupts emotional autopilot.
18. Compassion creates space for healing.
19. Alternatives must feel soothing to be effective.
20. You can learn to comfort yourself without financial consequences.

5 Trauma-Informed Soothing Techniques

1. Breathwork: The Slow-Exhale Method

Inhale for 4, exhale for 6.
Lowers cortisol and calms urgency within 90 seconds.

2. Grounding: The 5-4-3-2-1 Sensory Anchor

Name 5 things you see, 4 hear, 3 touch, 2 smell, 1 taste.
Brings the mind back to the present and stops overwhelm.

3. Sensory Reset: Cold Water on Wrists

Hold your wrists under cold water for 10 seconds.
This shocks the nervous system out of panic mode.

4. Pressure Point Technique

Press the center of your chest with two fingers for 10 seconds.
Stimulates vagus nerve relaxation.

5. Rhythmic Movement

Rock gently, sway, or tap your feet.
Replicates childhood soothing patterns and lowers adrenaline.

"Soothing Without Spending" Menu

- A warm drink
- Turning on soft lights
- Playing one comforting song
- A short walk
- A weighted blanket
- Slow stretching
- Calling a safe person
- Journaling
- Aromatherapy
- Cleaning one small area
- Putting hands under warm or cold water
- Watching calming videos
- Sitting outside for fresh air

Exercises:

Exercise 1: The Emotional Check-In Before Buying

Write down:

- What emotion am I feeling?
- What triggered it?
- What do I hope this purchase will fix?

Repeat before every purchase for one week.

Exercise 2: Body Scan for Spending Urges

Close your eyes and scan your body from head to toe.
Mark where discomfort shows up (chest tightness, stomach drop, throat tension).
This separates physical sensation from financial impulse.

Exercise 3: The 90-Second Delay

Set a 90-second timer when you want to buy something.
During those 90 seconds, breathe slowly.
If the urge fades, it was emotional. If it persists, evaluate with clarity.

The Soothing Substitution Ritual

Purpose: Replace spending with emotional regulation

Time: 5 minutes

1. **Pause & Place Hands on Heart**
   Say: "I am here with my feelings."
2. **Name the Emotion**
   Speak it aloud.
   Naming reduces limbic activation.
3. **Engage a Sensory Tool**
   Choose one from the menu: cold water, warm drink, music, grounding.
4. **Ask the Transformation Question**
   "What am I trying to feel right now? What am I trying to avoid?"
5. **Close with Safety Phrase**
   "I am allowed to soothe myself in ways that don't harm me."

This ritual rewires the emotional pathway that leads to spending.

Meditation: The Urge as a Wave

Close your eyes and imagine the urge to shop as a wave rising slowly in your chest.
Don't fight it—just watch it.
Feel it rise, peak, and fall.
Observe that the wave always softens.
End with: "I can feel this without spending."

10 Journal Prompts

1. What emotion am I trying to quiet before I shop?
2. What does shopping replace in my life?
3. When do I feel the strongest urges to buy something?
4. What does "comfort" mean to my body?
5. What pain am I trying to interrupt by spending?
6. What did soothing look like in my childhood?
7. What makes me feel emotionally unsafe?
8. How do I know when I'm emotionally overwhelmed?
9. What objects do I buy most when I'm stressed, and why?
10. What non-financial things comfort me deeply?

Closing Reflection

Shopping has carried the weight of your emotional world for years—sometimes decades. It has been the bridge between unbearable feelings and temporary relief. But now, with new tools, new awareness, and a new compassionate lens, you are learning to soothe without sacrificing your peace. Chapter 2 marks the moment you begin reclaiming your emotional life from the trauma that shaped it. You are not losing comfort—you are discovering real comfort.

Chapter 3: The Aftermath of Emotional Buying

The Emotional Hangover: What Happens After the Purchase

The moment after an emotional purchase can feel like silence after a storm. The dopamine high fades quickly, sometimes within minutes, leaving the nervous system without the artificial calm it relied on. This rapid shift often feels like a crash—a sudden heaviness, a sinking sensation in the chest, or a fog that settles in the mind. What felt soothing now feels confusing. What felt like comfort now feels like a mistake. This emotional hangover is not failure—it is chemistry.

During a trauma-spending episode, the brain temporarily shuts down long-term thinking and activates short-term relief. But once the purchase is complete, the prefrontal cortex comes back online. Logic returns. Reality returns. And with it comes a flood of self-awareness that feels overwhelming. Many people describe the aftermath as "waking up" and realizing they were acting from pain, not intention. This creates internal chaos that is intensely uncomfortable.

The emotional hangover often includes self-criticism, embarrassment, or regret. This happens because the nervous system shifts from relief back into the original emotional state—overwhelm, abandonment wounds, anxiety, shame, or loneliness—plus the new layer of judgment. Instead of healing, the brain now sees two "problems": the original emotion and the outcome of the spending itself. This dual stress amplifies the emotional crash.

This cycle is deeply human. It does not mean you lack discipline or intelligence. It means your brain sought relief the only way it knew how. Emotional hangovers are not proof that you are irresponsible—they are evidence that your nervous system has been operating in survival mode for far too long.

The Hidden Cost of Shame: How It Quietly Controls Your Financial Behaviors

Shame is one of the most powerful emotional forces in trauma-spending. Unlike guilt—"I made a mistake"—shame attacks identity: "I am the mistake." Shame tells you there is something wrong with you, and that message seeps into every financial behavior. After an emotional purchase, shame doesn't just critique the action; it critiques the person. It says: "You're broken. You're irresponsible. You never learn. You ruin everything." These internal attacks create emotional damage far greater than the purchase itself.

Shame thrives in silence and secrecy. When you hide purchases, delete emails, bury bags, or avoid bank statements, shame deepens. You feel like you're living a double life—one where you want to heal and one where you're terrified of being judged. This secrecy reinforces the belief that you are "bad," which is exactly what shame wants you to think. Trauma survivors often carry shame from childhood, long before shopping was even a behavior. Emotional buying becomes the modern expression of that old wound.

Shame blocks healing because it keeps you in survival mode. When you feel ashamed, your body believes it is unsafe. The nervous system activates defensiveness, emotional numbing, or dissociation. These states reduce your capacity to reflect clearly, set boundaries, or make compassionate changes. Shame shrinks your world into panic and regret. It convinces you that the only way to feel better is to do the very thing that caused the shame—spend again.

Shame is not accountability. Shame is emotional self-destruction. Accountability empowers you to change; shame tells you that change is impossible. True healing begins the moment you understand that shame is a wound—not wisdom.

Why Self-Blame Keeps the Cycle Alive

Self-blame is shame's younger sibling. It appears rational—"I did this to myself"—but in reality, it keeps you trapped in emotional punishment. After a trauma-spending episode, self-blame often feels like responsibility, but it's actually a form of self-attack that prevents growth. When you blame yourself, the nervous system interprets the internal conflict as danger. This heightens stress hormones and makes emotional regulation harder, not easier.

The subconscious mind learns through repetition. If every spending episode ends with harsh self-blame, the brain wires the connection: **"spending = self-hatred."** This emotional wiring creates a loop**. You spend → you crash → you blame yourself → you feel terrible → you seek relief → you spend again.** The cycle continues not because you are weak but because your brain believes spending is the only quick way out of the emotional distress self-blame creates.

Self-blame also prevents you from exploring root causes. When you attack yourself, you stop asking the important questions: "What emotion triggered this?" "What pain was I trying to soothe?" "What need went unmet?" Self-blame keeps the focus on punishment instead of growth. Healing requires curiosity, not condemnation.

The truth is this: self-blame feels like control, but it's actually captivity. It keeps you tied to a cycle that never had your best interests at heart. You do not heal by punishing the parts of you that were hurting. You heal by listening to them.

Shadow Spending: The Story You Tell Yourself After You Buy

Shadow spending is the emotional narrative created after a purchase. It's the story you tell yourself about what your spending "means." For trauma survivors, this story is rarely kind. It often sounds like: "I'm irresponsible," "I can't be trusted," "I'll always be like this," or "I don't deserve financial stability." These narratives attach identity to actions, reinforcing shame loops that deepen emotional reliance on spending.

Shadow spending also involves secrecy. Hiding purchases, deleting receipts, avoiding statements, or pretending you "forgot" what you bought are all signs of emotional fear—not malicious intent. These behaviors don't come from dishonesty; they come from trauma. The child who grew up fearing judgment, disappointment, or punishment is still alive inside the adult. Hiding purchases is an attempt to protect that inner child from shame.

The internal narrative becomes even louder when external pressures—family, partners, or society—reinforce the belief that spending is a moral failure. Trauma survivors often internalize these voices as part of their identity. Shadow spending turns a financial behavior into an emotional identity crisis. You become both the judge and the defendant, creating a mental courtroom that never closes.

When you understand shadow spending, you reclaim power. You realize that the story you tell yourself after buying is often older than you are. It is rooted in old wounds, not current realities. And once you name the narrative, you can rewrite it.

The Neurochemical Crash: Understanding the Biology of Regret

After the dopamine spike from a purchase fades, the brain experiences a neurological drop similar to withdrawal. The prefrontal cortex (responsible for logic, planning, and long-term thinking) reactivates, and suddenly the person becomes hyper-aware of the purchase. This cognitive return creates an emotional crash. The body shifts from relief into regret, confusion, or panic. This shift is chemistry—not character.

Serotonin levels also drop, leading to low mood, irritability, or hopelessness. Cortisol rises again, overwhelming the nervous system with stress. This sudden neurochemical shift creates the emotional hangover feeling—heaviness, sadness, nausea, or numbness. Trauma survivors often misinterpret this crash as moral failure. But what they're really experiencing is the body recalibrating after an artificial high.

These biochemical patterns explain why accountability is impossible during the crash. The brain is not in a learning state—it is in a protective state. This is why attempts to "fix everything immediately"—budgeting frantically, overcorrecting, swearing off spending forever—don't work. The nervous system needs regulation before reasoning.

Understanding the biology behind regret creates a gentler path forward. The emotional crash is part of the cycle—not an indictment of your worth. You are not broken; your brain is recalibrating.

Breaking the Shame Myth: Accountability Does Not Require Suffering

Many trauma survivors believe that feeling shame after spending is responsible, mature, or corrective. But shame has never created sustainable change. Shame paralyzes, freezes, and isolates. It floods the body with self-hatred and fear, making emotional regulation impossible. Healing requires accountability, but accountability is clarity—not suffering.

Accountability sounds like: "I see what happened. I understand why it happened. I can respond differently next time." Shame sounds like: "I'm a failure. I'll never be different. I ruin everything." One opens the door to growth. The other slams it shut. True accountability is rooted in understanding, not punishment.

This chapter normalizes the aftermath of emotional buying and teaches you tools to detox from shame rather than drown in it. Shame is not your guide; it is your wound. And wounds need healing, not humiliation. You are allowed to acknowledge your spending patterns without attacking yourself. You are allowed to heal without suffering.

This is the moment you declare that shame has no role in your transformation. You are choosing a different way.

20 Lessons

1. Regret after spending is biology, not morality.
2. Shame hijacks healing.
3. Emotional hangovers are normal for trauma survivors.
4. Purchases do not define character.
5. Self-blame reinforces trauma loops.
6. Shadow spending is learned, not inherent.
7. Secrecy is a symptom of fear, not deception.
8. The emotional aftermath is an invitation to heal.
9. You cannot punish your way into change.
10. Neurochemical crashes mimic withdrawal.
11. Clarity returns only after regulation.
12. Shame isolates; accountability empowers.
13. Trauma survivors deserve gentleness.
14. Regret is not proof of failure.
15. Emotional impulses require compassion.
16. Old wounds fuel modern spending patterns.
17. Every healing attempt rewires your brain.
18. You can repair without suffering.
19. Relief-driven purchases do not reflect your worth.
20. Healing begins when shame ends.

TOOLS

Shame Detox Journaling Exercise
Write down:

1. What triggered the spending episode?
2. What emotion was I trying to soothe?
3. What story am I telling myself about this purchase?
4. Whose voice does this story sound like?
5. What is a kinder, truer story I can tell instead?

Repeat after every significant spending impulse or episode.

Step-by-Step Repair Ritual After a Spending Episode

1. **Pause and Ground**
   Place your hand on your chest and breathe slowly.
   Say: "I am safe. I can repair without punishment."
2. **Name the Emotion Beneath the Purchase**
   Identify the primary wound—loneliness, overwhelm, shame, fear, exhaustion.
3. **Bring the Nervous System Back Online**
   Do a grounding technique: sensory reset, tapping, cold water, or breathwork.
4. **Return to Compassion**
   Speak aloud: "I am healing, not failing."
5. **Take One Repair Action**
   Examples:
   - Log the purchase without judgment
   - Move the item to a neutral place
   - Revisit your emotional budget
   - Complete the reframing worksheet

This ritual restores your sense of safety and clarity.

Self-Compassion Script

Place your hand over your heart and repeat slowly:

"I am not my mistakes.
I am not my impulses.
I am not my past.
I am learning to soothe myself with love instead of fear.
I forgive the parts of me that were hurting.
I am growing in ways I cannot yet see.
I deserve compassion in every step of my healing."

Reframing Worksheet: What I Bought vs. What I Was Trying to Feel

What I Bought	Emotion I Felt	What I Was Trying to Feel Instead	A Healthier Way to Meet That Need
Example: New shoes	Over-whelmed	Relief and control	Breathwork + grounding

Fill this out for any emotional purchase.

Meditation: Holding the Aftermath With Kindness

Close your eyes and imagine the regret in your chest as a small, trembling child.

Instead of scolding them, imagine wrapping them in a warm blanket.

Say: "You were trying to feel safe. I understand. I'm here now."

Let the child soften in your arms.

Feel your breath deepen as compassion expands.

10 Journal Prompts

1. What emotion hits me first after emotional spending?
2. Whose voice do I hear when I criticize myself?
3. What part of me was trying to feel safe?
4. What fear shows up strongest in the aftermath?
5. What would compassion sound like instead of shame?
6. What need went unmet before the purchase?
7. What is the story I tell myself afterward?
8. How old does this shame feel?
9. What would accountability look like without guilt?
10. What truth do I want to tell myself moving forward?

Closing Reflection

The aftermath of emotional buying is not where your story ends—it is where your real healing begins. Every regret, every crash, every moment of shame is an opportunity to rewrite the narrative with compassion. You are not meant to drown in self-blame; you are meant to rise with clarity and gentleness. The emotional hangover is simply your body asking for a different kind of comfort—one rooted in safety, presence, and truth. As you learn to detox shame and embrace understanding, you reclaim your power, one tender moment at a time.

Chapter 4: Compassion-First Spending Detox

Detangling Your Identity From Your Purchasing Habits

Many trauma survivors unconsciously merge their identity with their spending patterns. When emotional buying becomes a long-term coping mechanism, it eventually becomes self-defining. You begin to believe that you *are* the "shopper," the "spender," the "irresponsible one," or the "person who never gets it right." But the truth is this: **you bought things to survive, not because you are irresponsible.** Your purchases were emotional life jackets—tools used to stay afloat when the world felt overwhelming or unsafe.

Identity detangling requires separating *who you are* from *what you did to cope.* You are not your patterns—you are the person who endured circumstances that shaped those patterns. When you begin to understand this, the shame that once felt heavy begins to loosen. Compassion becomes the lens through which you view your past spending choices. Those choices were not character flaws; they were emotional signals. They were messages from your nervous system saying: "I need comfort."

Trauma creates emotional identities around shopping. For example, **The Back-to-School Fixer** spends money to recreate the childhood stability they never had. **The Holiday Healer** buys gifts to compensate for emotional wounds left by chaotic or lonely holidays. **The New-Version-of-Me Spender** buys tools, outfits, or self-improvement items to escape the version of themselves shaped by trauma. These identities are not failures—they are survival strategies. But they are not the truth of who you are. They are emotional roles.

Identity detangling is the first step toward healing. It is an act of reclaiming your narrative. It allows you to say: "My worth is not tied to my purchases. My identity is not defined by my coping mechanisms. I am more than my past patterns." When you separate identity from behavior, you create space for transformation rooted in self-love—not self-punishment.

Compassion-First Detox: Healing Without Deprivation or Shame

Traditional financial advice promotes restriction, self-blame, and discipline, but trauma survivors cannot heal through deprivation. A compassion-first spending detox rejects shame-based budgeting and embraces emotional healing. Instead of telling yourself "Stop buying everything!" you learn to ask, "What emotional need was I trying to meet?" This shift replaces control with understanding, and understanding with empowerment.

A compassion-first detox is not about preventing spending—it's about transforming the emotional impulse beneath it. No deprivation. No shaming budgets. No all-or-nothing thinking. Trauma survivors need safety and choice in order to heal, not punishment. When deprivation is used as a strategy, the nervous system becomes reactive, panicked, and overwhelmed—and the urge to spend increases. Healing requires stability, not scarcity.

Compassion-based financial healing involves treating every spending impulse like a message from your inner child. Punishment teaches fear, but compassion teaches awareness. Instead of forcing yourself into rigid financial rules, you learn flexible regulation tools that gently reduce emotional buying while supporting your wellbeing. Instead of saying, "I can't spend," the detox teaches you to say, "I can choose differently without hurting myself."

This chapter introduces gentle, loving strategies that help you rebuild trust with yourself and your money. You are not being deprived—you are being supported. You are not being controlled—you are being guided. A compassion-first detox honors your emotional history while helping you create safer pathways forward.

Rebuilding Emotional Regulation Without Shopping

To heal trauma-spending, the nervous system must learn to regulate without relying on purchases. Emotional regulation is not about suppressing feelings; it is about creating enough internal safety to *experience* feelings without being overwhelmed by them. The goal is not to eliminate emotional discomfort but to expand your capacity to hold it. When you can sit with emotions instead of fleeing from them, spending loses its power.

Nervous-system anchoring helps bring the body back into safety. This includes grounding techniques, slow breathing, muscle relaxation, or sensory resets. These tools teach the brain that safety can be created internally—not purchased externally. When the nervous system feels regulated, the urge to spend naturally reduces because the emotional alarm system quiets down.

Urge surfing is another powerful trauma-informed tool. Instead of fighting the desire to spend or giving in to it, you learn to *ride* the urge like a wave. The urge rises, peaks, and then falls. When you surf the wave instead of resisting or acting on it, the urge loses its intensity. You show your brain: "I can feel this and survive it." This breaks the automatic connection between discomfort and spending.

Measured delay methods create space between impulse and action. A delay of even 60–120 seconds can re-engage the prefrontal cortex and shift the emotional state enough to make a different choice. Trauma-safe decision-making means choices rooted in self-care rather than panic, fear, avoidance, or shame. With these tools, emotional regulation becomes a skill—not a struggle.

Trauma-Informed Strategies for Reducing Spending

Trauma-informed spending reduction is based on safety, gentleness, and clarity. It rejects financial shame and replaces it with emotional truth. The goal is not to restrict yourself—it is to retrain your brain to feel safe without constant purchasing. Trauma-informed strategies meet the nervous system where it is, not where the world expects it to be.

One strategy is **micro-delays**, where you delay a purchase by a short, manageable amount of time. While traditional financial programs suggest 30 days, trauma survivors benefit from 30 seconds to 10 minutes. These micro-delays help your nervous system adjust gradually rather than forcing an overwhelming shift. Small wins build confidence and create lasting change.

Another strategy is **needs vs. numbness clarity work.** Before a purchase, ask, "Is this buying comfort or solving a problem?" Naming the intention breaks emotional autopilot. If it's comfort, switch to an emotional regulation tool. If it's a practical need, proceed with awareness. The goal is to give yourself options—not pressure.

Lastly, trauma-informed reduction honors boundaries that feel loving, not punitive. "I don't buy when I'm overwhelmed" is a loving boundary. "I'm not allowed to buy anything ever again" is punishment. Trauma survivors need boundaries that help them feel held, not attacked. A gentle boundary is a supportive container that protects your healing—not a cage that suffocates it.

Loving Boundaries and the Shift From Shame to Self-Worth

The most powerful spending boundary is one rooted in self-worth. When you believe you are worthy of safety, stability, and emotional peace, your financial decisions shift naturally. Loving boundaries are not about restriction—they are about self-protection. They are a declaration that you deserve better than impulsive healing tools that hurt you afterward.

Loving boundaries focus on emotional safety first. For example:

- "I pause when I feel emotionally overwhelmed."
- "I check in with my body before I spend."
- "I soothe myself before making a decision."
- "I don't spend to escape loneliness—I seek support instead."

These boundaries hold you gently while you learn healthier ways of managing discomfort.

Shame-based limits sound like: "I can't be trusted," "I always ruin things," or "I have no discipline." These boundaries recreate the emotional neglect and criticism you experienced in childhood. They activate the same wounds that triggered your trauma-spending in the first place. Loving boundaries do the opposite—they nurture the child within you who once felt unsafe.

As you rebuild your internal narrative, you begin speaking to yourself differently. You shift from "What's wrong with me?" to "What happened to me?" and "How can I support myself right now?" You begin to see yourself as someone worthy of care, not correction. This shift rebuilds self-worth from the ground up.

Shifting Internal Narratives: Healing the Way You Speak to Yourself About Money

Internal narratives shape every financial decision you make. If you believe you are irresponsible or broken, you will spend to cope with the pain of that belief. If you believe you are capable, deserving, and healing, your choices will reflect that truth. Shifting the narrative around money and worth is one of the most transformative steps in trauma-spending recovery.

Begin by identifying your core money story. Many trauma survivors internalize harmful messages in childhood such as: "There's never enough," "I'm a burden," or "I can't ask for what I need." These stories fuel emotional spending because they create chronic internal scarcity. Changing your story means retraining your brain: "I deserve stability," "I can learn new skills," "I can handle discomfort," and "I am becoming stronger."

Narrative healing is gradual. Every time you speak kindly to yourself after a spending impulse, you create a new neural pathway. Every time you regulate instead of spending, you rewrite the narrative. Every time you choose compassion over criticism, you strengthen your emotional resilience. Healing is not dramatic—it is consistent, gentle repetition.

When you shift your narrative, your financial identity changes. You stop seeing yourself as someone who "can't change" and start seeing yourself as someone who *is* changing. You stop being the villain in your own financial story and start becoming the hero who learns new tools, builds new habits, and treats themselves with the love they always deserved.

20 Lessons

1. Your spending habits are not your identity.
2. You can change without punishing yourself.
3. Compassion heals patterns shame cannot.
4. Emotional safety is the foundation of financial clarity.
5. Delays create space for mindful choices.
6. Urge surfing teaches emotional resilience.
7. You are not irresponsible—you adapted.
8. Healthy boundaries nurture, not restrict.
9. Choices rooted in panic are not true choices.
10. Regulation tools reduce impulsive spending.
11. Your financial identity can be rewritten.
12. Emotional needs deserve attention—not avoidance.
13. Gentleness builds trust with yourself.
14. Internal narratives shape behavior.
15. Identity detangling frees you from shame.
16. You can soothe without spending.
17. Every compassionate choice rewires your brain.
18. You deserve stability and peace.
19. You are capable of transformation.
20. Healing is a practice, not perfection.

TOOLS

7-Day Compassion Spending Detox

Day 1: Awareness Without Judgment
Track a spending impulse without acting on it. Simply observe.

Day 2: Emotional Naming
Before any purchase, write the emotion underneath it.

Day 3: Replace One Purchase With One Regulation Tool
Cold water, grounding, music, journaling—anything soothing.

Day 4: Shadow Identity Recognition
Identify a spending identity ("Holiday Healer," etc.) and write its origins.

Day 5: Micro-Delay Practice
Delay every non-essential purchase by 3 minutes.

Day 6: Nervous System Anchoring
Use breathwork or grounding when an urge hits.

Day 7: Rebuilding Self-Trust
Write a letter to your future self: "I am learning. I am healing."

Urge Surfing Script (Trauma-Informed)

1. Sit comfortably and breathe slowly.
2. Imagine the urge as a wave rising in your body.
3. Say: "This is a feeling, not an emergency."
4. Let the wave rise without reacting.
5. Observe the peak: "I can survive this moment."
6. Watch the wave fall naturally.
7. End with: "I choose safety over urgency."

Identity Detangling Worksheet

Spending Identity	What It Represents Emotionally	Childhood Root	What I Actually Needed
Back-to-School Fixer	Trying to create stability	Chaos/neglect	Emotional safety
Holiday Healer	Trying to rewrite old pain	Lonely holidays	Connection
New-Version-of-Me Spender	Escaping trauma identity	Low self-worth	Self-acceptance

Fill out your own identities and rewrite what you truly needed.

"Pause–Plan–Proceed" Method for Purchases

1. **Pause**
   Stop for 20–60 seconds. Breathe.
2. **Plan**
   Ask:
   - "What emotion is present?"
   - "Is this a need or a numbing tool?"
   - "Will I still want this tomorrow?"
3. **Proceed**
   Move forward with clarity—not emotion.

Meditation: Becoming the Safe Place

Sit comfortably and close your eyes.
Place one hand over your heart and breathe slowly.
Say: “I am the safe place I have been searching for.”
Visualize a soft light in your chest expanding outward.
With each inhale, imagine that light growing.
With each exhale, imagine shame dissolving.
End with: “I can choose differently because I am worthy.”

10 Journal Prompts

1. What identity have I tied to my spending habits?
2. What did that identity protect me from?
3. What does a loving boundary look like for me?
4. How do I want to speak to myself about money?
5. What emotion drives most of my spending impulses?
6. What is my biggest financial fear?
7. What does emotional safety feel like in my body?
8. What would healing—not restriction—look like?
9. What do I want my future spending habits to reflect?
10. Who am I becoming as I heal?

Closing Reflection

A compassion-first detox is not about taking away your comfort—it is about giving you real comfort for the first time. This chapter marks the moment you stop defining yourself by your patterns and start defining yourself by your healing. You are no longer the shadow of your past spending habits— you are the person choosing softness, clarity, and emotional safety. Every compassionate choice is a declaration: "I deserve better." And piece by piece, breath by breath, you are building a life where soothing doesn't cost your future.

Chapter 5: Building a Trauma-Healed Relationship With Money

Rebuilding Safety Around Money: Emotional Security Before Financial Strategy

Healing your relationship with money begins with rebuilding safety—not budgets, not spreadsheets, not rigid self-control. For trauma survivors, financial safety is an emotional experience before it is a practical one. If money has ever been tied to fear, instability, shame, uncertainty, or survival-mode thinking, the nervous system interprets financial decisions as danger signals. Before you can regulate your finances, you must regulate your body's response to them. Emotional safety makes room for clarity.

Money dysregulation often emerges from environments where money was unpredictable—either scarce, controlled, chaotic, or used as a tool of manipulation. The nervous system learned early on that money is a threat, not a resource. This wiring continues into adulthood, creating panic around bills, avoidance around budgeting, or impulsive spending to escape fear. Rebuilding financial safety means teaching your body a new language: "Money is information, not danger." You cannot think clearly about money when your body feels unsafe.

Financial safety develops when you build consistency—small, predictable actions practiced without shame. Looking at your bank balance without judgment. Paying a bill without panic. Making a spending decision without emotional collapse. These small experiences teach the nervous system that money can be engaged with gently. Over time, money becomes a neutral tool instead of a trigger.

When emotional safety is in place, the financial strategies become easier and more effective. Budgeting no longer feels like punishment. Saving no longer feels like restriction. Planning no longer feels like a threat. When your nervous system feels steady, your financial decisions become grounded, compassionate, and sustainable.

Rebuilding Self-Worth Without Purchases: Becoming More Than What You Buy

Trauma often teaches the subconscious mind that worth must be proven, performed, or purchased. Many survivors learned early on that approval came from achievement, appearance, or objects—not from inherent worthiness. Emotional spending becomes a way to recreate that external sense of value: "If I have this, I will feel good enough." But self-worth built on purchases is fragile—it collapses as soon as the dopamine fades.

Rebuilding self-worth requires disentangling your identity from your possessions. You are not what you buy, what you own, or what you can afford. Your worth is intrinsic, not transactional. Healing begins when you stop using spending to validate your existence and start cultivating internal worthiness through emotional, psychological, and spiritual practices. You learn to affirm yourself in ways money never could.

This process involves acknowledging the parts of you that once sought love, acceptance, or visibility through purchases. These parts were not "bad"—they were trying to fill emotional voids left by neglect, rejection, or instability. When you approach these parts with compassion instead of judgment, you begin to strengthen your inner foundation. The less you depend on purchases for self-worth, the more empowered you feel.

Self-worth without spending is revolutionary for trauma survivors. It means you no longer need to buy your identity—you can build it. You no longer need to buy your comfort—you can cultivate it. You no longer need to buy your worth—you can embody it. This is the moment you reclaim the truth: **your value has never been for sale.**

Healthy Financial Self-Regulation: Learning Balance, Awareness, and Emotional Grounding

Healthy self-regulation isn't about strict budgets—it's about emotional grounding. Trauma-healed financial self-regulation means navigating spending impulses, financial decisions, and emotional triggers with steadiness instead of panic. Regulation is what allows you to make choices based on intuition and clarity rather than fear or urgency.

Somatic money practices help reconnect the body and financial decisions. These practices may include placing a hand on your chest before spending, breathing deeply before reviewing accounts, or grounding yourself physically before making choices. These tiny rituals retrain your brain: financial decisions can be calm and embodied.

Self-regulation also means distinguishing between **safe spending** and **soothing spending**. Safe spending supports your life—food, bills, tools, self-care, and intentional enjoyment. Soothing spending attempts to regulate emotions—loneliness, stress, shame, rejection, or anxiety. When you learn to identify the difference, you regain control over your financial narrative. You are no longer reacting—you are responding.

Scarcity scripts—internal beliefs such as "there's never enough," "I can't trust myself," or "I'll lose everything"—can be rewired through consistent regulation. When your nervous system learns safety, your brain rewires scarcity into sufficiency. This shift builds a healthier dopamine system. You no longer rely on shopping for reward; you begin finding reward in stability, success, and emotional peace.

Creating a Long-Term Trauma-Informed Money Ecosystem

A trauma-informed money ecosystem is a compassionate, sustainable financial environment built around safety, clarity, and emotional truth. It's not a budget—it's a lifestyle. It recognizes your lived experiences and supports your healing long-term. This ecosystem includes trauma-safe spending rules, emotional check-ins, safe saving practices, and boundaries around emotional triggers.

This ecosystem is flexible, not rigid. Trauma survivors cannot thrive in restrictive systems—they need adaptable frameworks that honor their emotional rhythms. This might mean having a small "comfort fund" for days when emotional support is needed. It may mean using visual tools instead of spreadsheets. It may involve tracking triggers instead of transactions. A trauma-informed money ecosystem meets you where you are.

A long-term system also includes rebuilding a healthy reward system. Instead of getting dopamine from purchases, you begin creating dopamine through accomplishment, connection, rest, creativity, body regulation, learning, or nature. These practices strengthen emotional independence and weaken the spending impulse. You are training your brain to feel rewarded by life—not objects.

The ultimate goal is not perfection. It is not becoming someone who "never spends emotionally again." The goal is a regulated relationship with money—one where financial decisions align with your values, emotions feel manageable, and your future feels safe. A trauma-informed money ecosystem supports your healing not for a week, a month, or a season—but for a lifetime.

Becoming the Regulated Spender, the Self-Trusting Adult, and the Emotionally Wealthy Person

Healing your relationship with money is ultimately healing your relationship with yourself. You become the **regulated spender** when financial decisions come from calm rather than panic. You become the **self-trusting adult** when you believe in your ability to make safe, grounded choices. You become the **emotionally wealthy person** when your internal world feels stable, abundant, and enough.

Becoming the regulated spender means you no longer rely on chaos to make decisions. You pause, breathe, anchor, and choose with clarity. Money becomes a collaborator, not an enemy. Purchases become intentional, not impulsive. Your spending becomes aligned with your values, not your wounds.

Becoming the self-trusting adult is the deepest transformation. Trauma steals trust—trust in the world, trust in people, trust in stability, and trust in yourself. Rebuilding self-trust means showing up consistently, gently, and compassionately. It means believing that you can handle feelings without numbing them. It means knowing you can repair financial mistakes without self-destruction.

Becoming emotionally wealthy means recognizing that wealth is not money—it is regulation, peace, fulfillment, and connection. It is feeling safe in your body, grounded in your identity, and confident in your choices. Emotional wealth lasts longer than any purchase. It is the abundance that trauma could not take from you.

The Path Forward: Progress, Not Perfection

Healing trauma-spending is not about perfection—it is about progress. The nervous system heals through repetition, consistency, and gentleness—not through rigid rules or impossible goals. You will have days when emotional spending urges return. You will have moments where old patterns try to resurface. This is not failure—it is memory. Healing is not linear. It spirals, circles, expands, contracts, and moves at your pace.

The path forward includes accepting setbacks as part of the journey. When you respond to regression with compassion instead of shame, you grow stronger. Each time you regulate instead of panic, pause instead of react, or reflect instead of judge, you rewrite your emotional wiring. These small victories accumulate, slowly reshaping your identity and your financial habits.

You do not need to heal perfectly to heal effectively. You do not need to become someone who "never struggles again." You only need to become someone who honors their emotions, regulates their nervous system, and chooses compassion over punishment. That is enough. More than enough.

The path ahead is yours to walk with gentleness, strength, and clarity. You are not repairing a broken system—you are building a new one.

20 Lessons

1. Emotional safety is the foundation of financial clarity.
2. Self-worth cannot be purchased.
3. Somatic money practices change emotional wiring.
4. Safe spending differs from soothing spending.
5. Scarcity scripts can be rewritten.
6. Dopamine can be healed without purchases.
7. Trusting yourself is a financial skill.
8. Regulation precedes wise financial decisions.
9. Trauma-informed systems last longer than willpower.
10. Money is a tool, not a threat.
11. Setbacks are part of healing, not proof of failure.
12. You can build a new financial identity.
13. Emotional wealth outlasts material wealth.
14. Consistency matters more than perfection.
15. Loving boundaries create safety.
16. You can learn to feel before you spend.
17. You can soothe without buying.
18. You are capable of financial peace.
19. Healing happens in small, compassionate steps.
20. You are becoming someone you can trust.

TOOLS

Trauma-Healed Money Rituals

1. The Morning Safety Ritual

- Place a hand on your heart.
- Speak aloud: "Money is information, not danger."
- Breathe slowly for 60 seconds.

This trains your nervous system to feel safe before daily financial decisions.

2. The Intentional Spending Ritual

Before a purchase, ask:

- "What do I feel?"
- "What do I need?"
- "What choice supports my healing?"

This reframes spending into empowerment.

3. The End-of-Day Repair Ritual

At night, write one sentence: "Today I am learning to trust myself." This rewires self-trust through repetition.

Emotional Budgeting Template (Trigger-Based)

Section 1: Emotional Triggers

- When I feel ____ I tend to spend on ____.
- When I feel ____ I avoid looking at my accounts.

Section 2: Safety Substitutions

- When triggered, I will regulate with ____ before spending.

Section 3: Intentional Categories

- Safe spending: groceries, bills, health, tools I use
- Soothing spending: emotional items
- Allowed comfort fund: $_____

Section 4: Check-In Questions

- “Is this a need?”
- “Is this a comfort?”
- “Is this an emotional escape?”

Self-Worth Rebuilding Practice

1. Sit comfortably and breathe slowly.
2. Place a hand on your chest.
3. Say aloud:
   "My worth is not measured by what I buy.
   My worth is not measured by what I earn.
   My worth is inherent, stable, and unshakeable."
4. Repeat twice daily for 14 days.

Meditation: Becoming Financially Safe

Close your eyes and breathe deeply.
Imagine standing in a warm, golden light that surrounds your body.
Say: “I am safe. My future is safe. My choices are mine.”
Feel the light flow into your chest, calming your heartbeat.
Imagine walking forward on a steady path lined with peace.
End with: “I am building a life I trust.”

10 Journal Prompts

1. What does financial safety feel like in my body?
2. What money fears are rooted in childhood?
3. What would safe spending mean for me?
4. What emotions trigger my spending most?
5. How can I build self-worth without purchases?
6. What does emotional wealth mean to me?
7. What scarcity scripts am I ready to retire?
8. How can I regulate before spending?
9. Who am I becoming as I heal financially?
10. What long-term money ecosystem feels compassionate and sustainable?

Closing Reflection: Stepping Into Financial Peace

Financial peace is not a destination—it is a relationship. A relationship built slowly, gently, and lovingly. You are not repairing old damage; you are creating new foundations. You are stepping into a version of yourself that is steady, grounded, and capable. A version of yourself who understands money as a tool, not a threat. A version who trusts their own choices. A version who knows they deserve safety, stability, and emotional abundance.

Your trauma did not break your relationship with money—it simply shaped it. Now, you are reshaping it with compassion. And with every breath, every pause, every intentional choice, you are becoming someone who walks toward financial peace with confidence and grace.

Appendix A: Spending Trigger Tracker

Understanding Spending Triggers: Your Nervous System's Early Warning System

Spending triggers are emotional, physical, social, or situational cues that activate the urge to buy. They often appear long before the conscious mind becomes aware of the desire to shop. For trauma survivors, these triggers are not random—they are conditioned responses shaped by lived experiences, unmet needs, and unresolved emotional patterns. Understanding your triggers means understanding the invisible language of your nervous system.

A trigger may be as obvious as a stressful argument or as subtle as a moment of boredom. It may be a memory, a conversation, a disappointment, an unmet expectation, or even a sensory experience like a smell, sound, or bodily sensation. Triggers are doorways into deeper emotional needs, and recognizing them creates the possibility for compassionate intervention. Once you know what activates the spending urge, you can redirect the emotional energy rather than fall into impulse.

Triggers are reflections of your emotional life. A spending urge may indicate loneliness, overwhelm, shame, fatigue, rejection, boredom, or the need to feel in control. Trauma survivors often misinterpret these urges as failures of discipline, when in reality, they are messages from the body: "I need soothing." The Spending Trigger Tracker helps you decode these messages in real time, transforming impulsive reactions into intentional responses.

Recognizing triggers is the foundation of emotional freedom. This appendix acts as your guide, your interpreter, and your partner in healing. By understanding your triggers, you begin to understand yourself—not as someone who overspends, but as someone who is learning what their inner world truly needs.

The Trigger Identification Method: A Step-by-Step Process

The Trigger Identification Method teaches you how to slow down the impulse and observe the emotional landscape beneath it. This method is designed to work even when you feel overwhelmed, numb, or reactive. It is trauma-sensitive, meaning it avoids shame and focuses on curiosity. You are not judging your triggers—you are naming them so you can support yourself differently.

Step one is **pause and notice**. When the urge to spend arises, even for a moment, pause. You do not need to change anything—just observe. Ask yourself: "What is happening inside me right now?" Notice your breathing, your posture, your thoughts, and your emotional sensations. The body always speaks first.

Step two is **identify the emotional root**. Is the urge connected to loneliness, irritation, stress, exhaustion, disappointment, insecurity, or boredom? Naming the emotion reduces its intensity. Trauma survivors often fear emotions because they were once overwhelming or unsafe, but naming emotions helps regulate the nervous system.

Step three is **identify the trigger source**. What happened before the urge arose? A conversation? A memory? A stressor? A long day? A social media comparison? Once you identify the trigger, you can understand what emotional need the spending impulse is attempting to soothe. This knowledge becomes power—not to control yourself, but to care for yourself.

The 30-Day Spending Trigger Tracking Grid

Tracking your triggers over 30 days helps you recognize patterns you didn't know existed. Many people are shocked to discover that their emotional spending urges appear at predictable times—after work, late at night, after specific family interactions, on weekends, or during loneliness spikes. A tracking grid transforms intuition into data. It creates emotional clarity.

Each entry includes:

- **Date & Time**
- **Trigger Type (emotional, physical, situational, relational)**
- **What happened before the urge?**
- **Emotion felt**
- **Intensity of urge (1–10)**
- **What I needed**
- **What action I chose instead**
- **Outcome**

This grid not only identifies patterns but also shows progress. Even if you still feel urges, you may notice they become less intense, less frequent, or easier to regulate. Healing is measured not by perfection but by increasing self-awareness and decreasing emotional urgency.

Over 30 days, the grid becomes a mirror reflecting your emotional life. You begin to see root themes—loneliness, stress, abandonment wounds, perfectionism, overwhelm, or the need for validation. These themes help you tailor your healing practices. You no longer see spending as random—you see it as conversation between you and your nervous system.

At the end of the 30 days, you review the grid to identify the most common triggers. Instead of reacting to them with shame, you treat them as invitations for deeper emotional care. This is how awareness becomes transformation.

The Trigger-Response Map: What Your Urges Are Trying to Tell You

Every spending urge communicates a need. The Trigger-Response Map helps you decode what the urge really means. Trauma survivors often suppress emotional needs or feel guilty for having them. The map helps you rebuild emotional fluency. It shows that the urge isn't the problem—the unmet need beneath it is.

For example, if the trigger is **loneliness**, the urge may say: "I need connection." If the trigger is **overwhelm**, the urge may say: "I need rest or support." If the trigger is **shame**, the urge may say: "I need compassion." By mapping the trigger to the underlying need, you learn that emotional spending was never about the purchase—it was about relief.

The Trigger-Response Map includes categories like:

- **Emotional triggers** (fear, sadness, rejection)
- **Physical triggers** (fatigue, hunger, sensory overload)
- ** situational triggers** (bills, family arguments, work stress)
- **Internal narratives** ("I'm not enough," "I deserve something nice," "I need a win today")

Once you identify the need, you can choose a healthier response. This transforms spending impulses into self-connection opportunities. Your nervous system stops relying on purchases to soothe pain because you learn to meet your needs directly.

Over time, this practice creates an internal sense of emotional safety. You begin responding to emotions instead of avoiding them. You become your own source of comfort.

The Trauma-Informed Decision Tree: Choosing With Clarity Instead of Urgency

This decision tree is designed to help you move from emotional reactivity to emotional clarity. It is not a budgeting tool—it is a nervous-system tool. Trauma survivors benefit from structured, predictable steps that gently guide them into regulated decision-making. The decision tree helps you slow down and assess without fear.

The first question is: **"Is this a need or a numb?"** Needs are functional. Numbs are emotional. This single question reactivates the prefrontal cortex, helping you step out of survival mode. The second question is: **"What emotion am I feeling?"** Naming the emotion reduces limbic activation. The third question is: **"What else can soothe me in this moment?"** This opens the door to regulated alternatives.

Next, you ask: **"Will I still want this tomorrow?"** Trauma survivors often struggle with future-thinking because survival-mode thinking is immediate. Pausing for 24 hours bypasses the impulse and gives space for clarity. If the purchase still feels aligned tomorrow, it may be intentional—not reactive.

Finally, the decision tree ends with: **"Does this support the life I am trying to build?"** This question connects you to your healed identity: the regulated spender, the self-trusting adult, the emotionally wealthy human being. This identity-oriented decision-making rewires your long-term financial patterns.

What This Trigger Is Really Saying: Emotional Decoder for Trauma Survivors

Every trigger has a hidden emotional message. This decoder helps you understand the deeper meaning beneath your urges. When you listen compassionately, you stop misinterpreting urges as problems and start seeing them as invitations to heal.

If the trigger is stress:
Your body is saying, "I feel unsafe. Help me calm down."

If the trigger is boredom:
Your mind is saying, "I need stimulation or creativity."

If the trigger is loneliness:
Your heart is saying, "I need connection."

If the trigger is shame:
Your inner child is saying, "I need forgiveness and compassion."

If the trigger is fatigue:
Your body is saying, "I need rest, not reward."

If the trigger is jealousy or comparison:
Your identity is saying, "I want growth, not objects."

If the trigger is rejection:
Your nervous system is saying, "I need reassurance and comfort."

This decoder transforms emotional chaos into emotional clarity. When you address the real need, the urge dissolves without a fight. You learn to become your own healer instead of relying on purchases to medicate emotional pain.

Trauma-Healed Tools

Trauma-Healed Money Rituals for Spending Triggers

1. The Emotional Check-In Ritual

Place your hand over your heart.
Say: "What am I actually feeling right now?"
Breathe slowly.
Let the answer come without judgment.

2. The Somatic Pause Ritual

Sit still.
Feel your feet on the ground.
Relax your jaw and shoulders.
Let your body return to safety before making a decision.

3. The Compassionate Naming Ritual

Say aloud:
"This feeling is temporary.
My safety is not determined by this urge.
I can choose differently with love."

Emotional Budgeting Template (Trigger-Based)

1. My Top Emotional Triggers:

- ______
- ______
- ______

2. How They Show Up in My Body:

- Tight chest
- Shallow breathing
- Numbness
- Restlessness

3. My Default Response Pattern:

- Browse → Buy → Relief → Shame

4. My New Compassion Responses:

- Breathe → Identify → Regulate → Decide

5. My Safe Spending Categories:

- Needs
- Intentional pleasure
- Long-term stability

6. My Emotional Red Flags:

- Buying to escape feelings
- Buying because of guilt
- Buying because of loneliness

Self-Worth Rebuilding Practice: Rewriting the Internal Money Narrative

1. Sit quietly with a hand on your heart.
2. Repeat:
   **"My worth is not tied to my purchases.
   My worth is not tied to my productivity.
   I am worthy because I exist."**
3. Breathe deeply and imagine your inner child hearing this for the first time.
4. Visualize them softening, trusting, releasing shame.
5. Repeat daily.

10 Journal Prompts

1. What event today triggered my urge to shop?
2. What emotion was beneath the trigger?
3. How intense was the urge (1–10)?
4. What did I truly need in that moment?
5. How did my body react?
6. What internal narrative arose?
7. What healthier option could have soothed me?
8. What did this trigger teach me about myself?
9. What pattern do I notice across multiple triggers?
10. How can I support myself more compassionately tomorrow?

Closing Reflection:

Learning the Language of Your Triggers

Your spending triggers are not enemies—they are communicators. Each one is a message from your inner child, your nervous system, and your emotional truth. They rise not to sabotage you, but to ask for support. They appear because a part of you is still healing. When you track them without shame, you begin speaking the language of your own heart.

As you learn this language, you no longer fear the urge to spend—you understand it. You soothe it. You hold it gently. And with that, the cycle changes. Your trigger becomes a moment of awareness. Awareness becomes choice. Choice becomes empowerment. And empowerment becomes peace.

You are not fighting against yourself anymore.
You are partnering with yourself.
That is the beginning of a trauma-healed relationship with money—and a trauma-healed life.

Appendix B: Emotional Buying to Mindful Earning

The Shift From Emotional Buying to Mindful Earning

Transitioning from emotional buying to mindful earning is not simply a financial pivot—it is an emotional and psychological evolution. Emotional buying often emerges from internal wounds: loneliness, shame, overwhelm, abandonment trauma, or the need to feel in control. Mindful earning emerges from healing, clarity, groundedness, and self-worth. This appendix guides you through transforming your relationship with money from reactive to intentional, from panic-driven to purpose-driven.

When you are caught in emotional buying cycles, money feels like a coping tool. It becomes something you use *against* discomfort rather than something you use *to build* stability. But earning—especially mindful earning—invites the opposite: money becomes a resource you create with clarity, creativity, self-trust, and emotional safety. Instead of being consumed by impulses, you begin generating income from a place of power.

Mindful earning requires emotional bandwidth. Trauma survivors often feel unsafe when thinking about money because earning may have been tied to pressure, expectations, or past failures. To truly shift into mindful earning, the nervous system must first believe that earning is safe. When earning is rooted in safety, self-worth, and alignment, your financial life becomes a reflection of healing—not survival mode.

This appendix helps you build a space where earning feels nourishing, not draining; expansive, not intimidating; empowering, not overwhelming. You are not just learning to earn—you are learning to earn from a healed identity.

Understanding the Emotional Mechanics Behind Buying and Earning

Emotional buying and mindful earning trigger different parts of the brain. Emotional buying activates the limbic system—the survival center. In this state, the brain seeks quick relief and immediate dopamine. Mindful earning activates the prefrontal cortex—the planning, visioning, problem-solving part of your mind. The shift begins when you learn to regulate the limbic system long enough for the prefrontal cortex to come back online.

The limbic system says: "I need comfort right now."
The prefrontal cortex says: "I can build comfort long-term."

Your goal is not to shame the limbic system but to soothe it. Emotional buying becomes a signal that the body is overwhelmed, not a sign of failure. When you comfort the limbic system with emotional tools, you free up cognitive space for creativity, grounded decision-making, and productive energy—exactly what mindful earning requires.

Earning also requires self-worth. Trauma often damages self-worth by making people believe they're not capable, deserving, or good enough. When emotional wounds inform your financial story, earning feels intimidating. But when you heal those wounds, earning becomes an expression of your power. You begin seeing money not as a threat, but as a partner.

The distinction between buying and earning becomes clearer: buying is temporary relief; earning is long-term empowerment. When the nervous system learns this difference, your financial identity transforms.

Building a Mindful Earning Framework: Safety, Clarity, Worthiness, Action

Mindful earning begins with emotional safety. Before you can earn consistently, your nervous system must feel that work, money, and productivity are not threats. Many trauma survivors associate work with burnout, criticism, or fear. To build mindful earning habits, you must first rebuild your nervous system's relationship to productivity. This includes rest, boundaries, and creating work rhythms that don't mirror past trauma.

The second pillar is clarity. Mindful earning comes from knowing what you want to create, what your strengths are, and what income paths feel aligned with your emotional, energetic, and lifestyle needs. Clarity eliminates chaotic decision-making and replaces it with intentional, values-driven earning.

The third pillar is worthiness. To earn mindfully, you must believe you deserve financial stability, success, support, and ease. Many trauma survivors unconsciously under-earn because they internalized beliefs such as "I'm not enough" or "I don't deserve more." Worthiness becomes the emotional backbone of mindful earning.

The fourth pillar is compassionate action. Mindful earning is not about productivity at all costs—it is about making consistent, self-honoring decisions. It is showing up for yourself without pushing yourself into survival mode. It is taking steps that honor your capacity, not imitate someone else's expectations.

Trauma-Safe Earning: Creating Work Habits That Don't Mirror Past Pain

A trauma-safe earning approach acknowledges something traditional financial advice ignores: **you cannot build abundance from a dysregulated nervous system.** Productivity rooted in fear, urgency, or shame burns you out and drives you back into emotional spending cycles. Trauma-safe earning means designing work habits that support healing rather than triggering survival mode.

First, trauma-safe earning honors emotional rhythms. Some days your nervous system has full capacity; other days it needs rest. Mindful earning recognizes that healing and productivity must coexist. Your value is not tied to output—it is tied to consistency and emotional alignment.

Second, trauma-safe earning avoids punishment-based motivational systems. Setting extreme goals, shaming yourself for slow progress, or forcing productivity creates collapse, not momentum. Trauma-informed earning encourages micro-actions, gentle pacing, and compassionate self-talk so your nervous system stays regulated.

Third, trauma-safe earning includes somatic grounding at the beginning and end of work periods. A 60-second grounding practice before you begin working can shift your nervous system into calm focus. Ending work with a regulation ritual helps prevent emotional spillover, making evenings calmer and spending urges weaker.

Finally, trauma-safe earning acknowledges that financial growth is not linear. You will have surges and pauses. Consistency matters more than intensity. Healing matters more than hustling. Your nervous system comes first.

Money-Identity Upgrade: Becoming the Builder, the Receiver, and the Emotionally Wealthy Earner

The emotional identity shift from emotional buyer to mindful earner is monumental. This shift is not just behavioral—it is identity-level transformation. You step into the role of **the Builder** when you create income intentionally instead of impulsively. You step into the role of **the Receiver** when you allow financial expansion without guilt. And you step into the role of **the Emotionally Wealthy Earner** when your worth no longer depends on purchases or productivity.

Becoming the Builder means trusting your capacity to create stability. It means recognizing your skills, ingenuity, resilience, and emotional intelligence as sources of income. Instead of relying on spending for emotional highs, you build systems that support long-term peace.

Becoming the Receiver means breaking internal barriers that reject abundance. Trauma survivors often self-sabotage because receiving feels unfamiliar or unsafe. When you let yourself receive money, opportunities, support, and ease, you step into a healed relational stance with abundance.

Becoming the Emotionally Wealthy Earner means redefining wealth as emotional regulation, stability, boundaries, aligned work, and self-worth. Emotional wealth creates financial wealth—not the other way around. When you embody emotional wealth, you stop chasing feelings through purchases and begin generating them through meaning, connection, creativity, and empowerment.

This identity upgrade marks the moment you stop surviving and start creating. You become the author of your financial life.

The Long-Term Ecosystem of Mindful Earning: Sustainable, Regulated Success

Mindful earning is a long-term ecosystem—not a short-term hustle. This ecosystem grows slowly, consistently, and compassionately. It includes habits, rituals, values, and emotional anchors that support your earning without overwhelming your nervous system.

This ecosystem includes structured rest, boundaries around work time, self-regulation practices, and intentional spending habits that keep your emotional world steady. As you create stability, emotional spending becomes rare—not because you forced yourself to stop, but because you no longer need it.

A mindful earning ecosystem also includes clear goals that reflect your values: impact, creativity, freedom, contribution, healing, or legacy—not fear. Goals aligned with safety feel energizing, not draining. They create momentum, not burnout.

Finally, the ecosystem includes community, support, learning, and financial growth through emotional growth. The healthier your nervous system becomes, the clearer and more consistent your earning becomes. Over time, the ecosystem becomes self-reinforcing: regulated emotions → mindful earning → financial stability → emotional safety → deeper regulation.

You are not just earning money.
You are building a life rooted in peace.

TOOLS

Mindful Earning Framework (4 Steps)

Step 1: Emotional Safety

Before working or planning, regulate your body. Breathe. Ground. Ask: "Is earning safe today?"

Step 2: Clarity Mapping

- What do I want to create?
- What strengths can I use?
- What income paths feel aligned?

Step 3: Worthiness Activation

Repeat daily:

"I deserve stability. I deserve abundance. I am capable of creating wealth."

Step 4: Compassionate Action

Take one aligned step. Not ten. Not perfect—one.

Value-Based Income Builder

1. List your skills.
2. Circle the skills that bring peace, joy, or meaning.
3. Identify small ways these can become income streams.
4. Choose the path that feels aligned—not intimidating.

Nervous-System Safe Earning Plan

Before working:

- 30 seconds deep breathing
- unclench jaw
- relax shoulders
- ground feet

During working:

- Work in 15–25 minute cycles
- Pause to breathe
- Avoid overwhelm cues

After working:

- Close laptop or step away
- Do 1–2 minutes of nervous-system repair
- Say: "I did enough."

Money-Identity Upgrade Map

Old Identity	New Identity	Emotional Shift
Emotional Buyer	Regulated Spender	From reaction to intention
Avoider	Self-Trusting Adult	From fear to clarity
Scarcity Survivor	Emotionally Wealthy Earner	From panic to empowerment

Trauma-Healed Productivity Ritual

1. Place a hand on your chest.
2. Say: "I can work gently, not urgently."
3. Set a tiny task.
4. Work for one cycle.
5. End with: "I choose stability over stress."

20 Lessons

1. Emotional buying is a survival response, not a flaw.
2. Mindful earning is built on emotional safety.
3. Trauma survivors need regulation, not pressure.
4. Worthiness is the foundation of sustainable income.
5. Emotional spending decreases when emotional safety increases.
6. Earning becomes easier when your nervous system feels safe.
7. Creativity expands when shame decreases.
8. Micro-actions build long-term financial strength.
9. Emotional wealth precedes financial wealth.
10. You can create income from alignment, not burnout.
11. Receiving money requires healing, not hustling.
12. Self-trust transforms your financial identity.
13. Clarity stops emotional chaos.
14. Scarcity scripts can be rewritten.
15. Nervous-system safe work habits prevent collapse.
16. Progress matters more than perfection.
17. Healthy boundaries protect your earning energy.
18. You deserve abundance that feels peaceful.
19. Mindful earning creates mindful living.
20. Healing your financial relationship heals your life.

10 Journal Prompts

1. What emotions usually lead to my buying impulses?
2. What would earning look like if it felt safe?
3. What skill or talent brings me peace and could become income?
4. What old money identity am I ready to release?
5. What new earning identity am I stepping into?
6. What beliefs about worthiness am I healing?
7. What earning patterns reflect trauma instead of truth?
8. How can I regulate my emotions before working?
9. What does emotional wealth mean to me today?
10. What small, mindful action can I take toward earning tomorrow?

Closing Reflection:

From Coping to Creating, From Surviving to Building

You are no longer living at the mercy of emotional buying cycles. You are becoming the conscious architect of your financial life. Mindful earning is not about hustle—it is about healing. It is about transforming emotional wounds into emotional wisdom, panic into peace, scarcity into sufficiency, and impulsive buying into intentional building.

You are learning to earn from a place of self-trust, emotional regulation, and alignment. You are no longer buying temporary relief—you are building long-term stability. You are no longer surviving your emotional world—you are shaping it.

This transformation is your birthright.

And this appendix marks the moment you step fully into it.

<u>Message from the Author:</u>

I hope you enjoyed this book, I love astrology and knew there was not a book such as this out on the shelf. I love metaphysical items as well. Please check out my other books:

-Life of Government Benefits

-My life of Hell

-My life with Hydrocephalus

-Red Sky

-World Domination:Woman's rule

-World Domination:Woman's Rule 2: The War

-Life and Banishment of Apophis: book 1

-The Kidney Friendly Diet

-The Ultimate Hemp Cookbook

-Creating a Dispensary(legally)

-Cleanliness throughout life: the importance of showering from childhood to adulthood.

-Strong Roots: The Risks of Overcoddling children

-Hemp Horoscopes: Cosmic Insights and Earthly Healing

- Celestial Hemp Navigating the Zodiac: Through the Green Cosmos

-Astrological Hemp: Aligning The Stars with Earth's Ancient Herb

-The Astrological Guide to Hemp: Stars, Signs, and Sacred Leaves

-Green Growth: Innovative Marketing Strategies for your Hemp Products and Dispensary

-Cosmic Cannabis

-Astrological Munchies

-Henry The Hemp

-Zodiacal Roots: The Astrological Soul Of Hemp

- **Green Constellations: Intersection of Hemp and Zodiac**

-Hemp in The Houses: An astrological Adventure Through The Cannabis Galaxy

-Galactic Ganja Guide

Heavenly Hemp

Zodiac Leaves

Doctor Who Astrology

Cannastrology

Stellar Satvias and Cosmic Indicas

Celestial Cannabis: A Zodiac Journey

AstroHerbology: The Sky and The Soil: Volume 1

AstroHerbology:Celestial Cannabis:Volume 2

Cosmic Cannabis Cultivation

The Starry Guide to Herbal Harmony: Volume 1

The Starry Guide to Herbal Harmony: Cannabis Universe: Volume 2

Yugioh Astrology: Astrological Guide to Deck, Duels and more

Nightmare Mansion: Echoes of The Abyss

Nightmare Mansion 2: Legacy of Shadows

Nightmare Mansion 3: Shadows of the Forgotten

Nightmare Mansion 4: Echoes of the Damned

The Life and Banishment of Apophis: Book 2

Nightmare Mansion: Halls of Despair

Healing with Herb: Cannabis and Hydrocephalus

Planetary Pot: Aligning with Astrological Herbs: Volume 1

Fast Track to Freedom: 30 Days to Financial Independence Using AI, Assets, and Agile Hustles

Cosmic Hemp Pathways

How to Become Financially Free in 30 Days: 10,000 Paths to Prosperity

Zodiacal Herbage: Astrological Insights: Volume 1

Nightmare Mansion: Whispers in the Walls

The Daleks Invade Atlantis

Henry the hemp and Hydrocephalus

10X The Kidney Friendly Diet

Cannabis Universe: Adult coloring book

Hemp Astrology: The Healing Power of the Stars

Zodiacal Herbage: Astrological Insights: Cannabis Universe: Volume 2

Planetary Pot: Aligning with Astrological Herbs: Cannabis Universes: Volume 2

Doctor Who: Convergence Protocol – The Replicator War

Nightmare Mansion: Curse of the Blood Moon

The Celestial Stoner: A Guide to the Zodiac

Cosmic Pleasures: Sex Toy Astrology for Every Sign

Hydrocephalus Astrology: Navigating the Stars and Healing Waters

Lapis and the Mischievous Chocolate Bar

Celestial Positions: Sexual Astrology for Every Sign

Apophis's Shadow Work Journal: **:** A Journey of Self-Discovery and Healing

Kinky Cosmos: Sexual Kink Astrology for Every Sign

Digital Cosmos: The Astrological Digimon Compendium

Stellar Seeds: The Cosmic Guide to Growing with Astrology

Apophis's Daily Gratitude Journal

Cat Astrology: Feline Mysteries of the Cosmos

The Cosmic Kama Sutra: An Astrological Guide to Sexual Positions

Unleash Your Potential: A Guided Journal Powered by AI Insights

Whispers of the Enchanted Grove

Cosmic Pleasures: An Astrological Guide to Sexual Kinks

369, 12 Manifestation Journal

Whisper of the nocturne journal(blank journal for writing or drawing)

The Boogey Book

Locked In Reflection: A Chastity Journey Through Locktober

Generating Wealth Quickly:How to Generate $100,000 in 24 Hours

Star Magic: Harness the Power of the Universe

The Flatulence Chronicles: A Fart Journal for Self-Discovery

The Doctor and The Death Moth

Seize the Day: A Personal Seizure Tracking Journal

The Ultimate Boogeyman Safari: A Journey into the Boogie World and Beyond

Whispers of Samhain: 1,000 Spells of Love, Luck, and Lunar Magic: Samhain Spell Book

Apophis's guides:Witch's Spellbook Crafting Guide for Halloween

Frost & Flame: The Enchanted Yule Grimoire of 1000 Winter Spells

The Ultimate Boogey Goo Guide & Spooky Activities for Halloween Fun

Harmony of the Scales: A Libra's Spellcraft for Balance and Beauty

The Enchanted Advent: 36 Days of Christmas Wonders

Nightmare Mansion: The Labyrinth of Screams

Harvest of Enchantment: 1,000 Spells of Gratitude, Love, and Fortune for Thanksgiving

The Boogey Chronicles: A Journal of Nightly Encounters and Shadowy Secrets

The 12 Days of Financial Freedom: A Step-by-Step Christmas Countdown to Transform Your Finances

Sigil of the Eternal Spiral Blank Journal

A Christmas Feast: Timeless Recipes for Every Meal

Holiday Stress-Free Solutions: A Survival Guide to Thriving During the Festive Season

Yu-Gi-Oh! Holiday Gifting Mastery: The Ultimate Guide for Fans and Newcomers Alike

Holiday Harmony: A Hydrocephalus Survival Guide for the Festive Season

Celestial Craft: The Witch's Almanac for 2025 – A Cosmic Guide to Manifestations, Moons, and Mystical Events

Doctor Who: The Toymaker's Winter Wonderland

Tulsa King Unveiled: A Thrilling Guide to Stallone's Mafia Masterpiece

Pendulum Craft: A Complete Guide to Crafting and Using Personalized Divination Tools

Nightmare Mansion: Santa's Eternal Eve

Starlight Noel: A Cosmic Journey through Christmas Mysteries

The Dark Architect: Unlocking the Blueprint of Existence

Surviving the Embrace: The Ultimate Guide to Encounters with The Hugging Molly

The Enchanted Codex: Secrets of the Craft for Witches, Wiccans, and Pagans

Harvest of Gratitude: A Complete Thanksgiving Guide

Yuletide Essentials: A Complete Guide to an Authentic and Magical Christmas

Celestial Smokes: A Cosmic Guide to Cigars and Astrology

Living in Balance: A Comprehensive Survival Guide to Thriving with Diabetes Insipidus

Cosmic Symbiosis: The Venom Zodiac Chronicles

The Cursed Paw of Ambition

Cosmic Symbiosis: The Astrological Venom Journal

Celestial Wonders Unfold: A Stargazer's Guide to the Cosmos (2024-2029)

The Ultimate Black Friday Prepper's Guide: Mastering Shopping Strategies and Savings

Cosmic Sales: The Astrological Guide to Black Friday Shopping

Legends of the Corn Mother and Other Harvest Myths

Whispers of the Harvest: The Corn Mother's Journal

The Evergreen Spellbook

The Doctor Meets the Boogeyman

The White Witch of Rose Hall's SpellBook

The Gingerbread Golem's Shadow: A Study in Sweet Darkness

The Gingerbread Golem Codex: An Academic Exploration of Sweet Myths

The Gingerbread Golem Grimoire: Sweet Magicks and Spells for the Festive Witch

The Curse of the Gingerbread Golem

10-minute Christmas Crafts for kids

Christmas Crisis Solutions: The Ultimate Last-Minute Survival Guide

Gingerbread Golem Recipes: Holiday Treats with a Magical Twist

The Infinite Key: Unlocking Mystical Secrets of the Ages

Enchanted Yule: A Wiccan and Pagan Guide to a Magical and Memorable Season

Dinosaurs of Power: Unlocking Ancient Magick

Astro-Dinos: The Cosmic Guide to Prehistoric Wisdom

Gallifrey's Yule Logs: A Festive Doctor Who Cookbook

The Dino Grimoire: Secrets of Prehistoric Magick

The Gift They Never Knew They Needed

The Gingerbread Golem's Culinary Alchemy: Enchanting Recipes for a Sweetly Dark Feast

A Time Lord Christmas: Holiday Adventures with the Doctor

Krampusproofing Your Home: Defensive Strategies for Yule

Silent Frights: A Collection of Christmas Creepypastas to Chill Your Bones

Santa Raptor's Jolly Carnage: A Dino-Claus Christmas Tale

Prehistoric Palettes: A Dino Wicca Coloring Journey

The Christmas Wishkeeper Chronicles

The Starlight Sleigh: A Holiday Journey

Elf Secrets: The True Magic of the North Pole

Candy Cane Conjurations

Cooking with Kids: Recipes Under 20 Minutes

Doctor Who: The TARDIS Confiscation

The Anxiety First Aid Kit: Quick Tools to Calm Your Mind

Frosty Whispers: A Winter's Tale

The Infinite Key: Unlocking the Secrets to Prosperity, Resilience, and Purpose

The Grasping Void: Why You'll Regret This Purchase

Astrology for Busy Bees: Star Signs Simplified

The Instant Focus Formula: Cut Through the Noise

The Secret Language of Colors: Unlocking the Emotional Codes

Sacred Fossil Chronicles: Blank Journal

The Christmas Cottage Miracle

Feeding Frenzy: Graboid-Inspired Recipes

Manifest in Minutes: The Quick Law of Attraction Guide

The Symbiote Chronicles: Doctor Who's Venomous Journey

Think Tiny, Grow Big: The Minimalist Mindset

The Energy Key: Unlocking Limitless Motivation

New Year, New Magic: Manifesting Your Best Year Yet

Unstoppable You: Mastering Confidence in Minutes

Infinite Energy: The Secret to Never Feeling Drained

Lightning Focus: Mastering the Art of Productivity in a Distracted World

Saturnalia Manifestation Magick: A Guide to Unlocking Abundance During the Solstice

Graboids and Garland: The Ultimate Tremors-Themed Christmas Guide

12 Nights of Holiday Magic

The Power of Pause: 60-Second Mindfulness Practices

The Quick Reset: How to Reclaim Your Life After Burnout

The Shadow Eater: A Tale of Despair and Survival

The Micro-Mastery Method: Transform Your Skills in Just Minutes a Day

Reclaiming Time: How to Live More by Doing Less

Chronovore: The Eternal Nexus

The Mind Reset: Unlocking Your Inner Peace in a Chaotic World
Confidence Code: Building Unshakable Self-Belief
Baby the Vampire Terrier
Baby the Vampire Terrier's Christmas Adventure
Celestial Streams: The Content Creator's Astrology Manual
The Wealth Whisperer: Unlocking Abundance with Everyday Actions
The Energy Equation: Maximize Your Output Without Burning Out
The Happiness Algorithm: Science-Backed Steps to Joyful Living
Stress-Free Success: Achieving Goals Without Anxiety
Mindful Wealth: The New Blueprint for Financial Freedom
The Festive Flavors of New Year: A Culinary Celebration
The Master's Gambit: Keys of Eternal Power
Shadowed Secrets: Groundhog Day Mysteries
Beneath the Burrow: Lessons from the Groundhog
Spring's Whispers: The Groundhog's Prediction
The Limitless Mindset: Unlock Your Untapped Potential
The Focus Funnel: How to Cut Through Chaos and Get Results
Bold Moves: Building Courage to Live on Your Terms
The Daily Shift: Simple Practices for Lasting Transformation
The Quarter-Life Reset: Thriving in Your 20s and 30s
The Art of Shadowplay: Building Your Own Personal Myth
The Eternal Loop: Finding Purpose in Repetition
Burrowing Wisdom: Life Lessons from the Groundhog
Shadow Work: A Groundhog Day Perspective
Love in Bloom: 5-Minute Romantic Gestures
The Shadowspell Codex: Secrets of Forbidden Magick
The Burnout Cure: Finding Balance in a Busy World
The Groundhog Prophecy: Unlocking Seasonal Secrets
Nog Tales: The Spirited History of Eggnog
Six More Weeks: Embracing Seasonal Transitions
The Lumivian Chronicles: Fragments of the Fifth Dimension

Money on Your Mind: A Beginner's Guide to Wealth
The Focus Fix: Breaking Through Distraction
January's Spirit Keepers: Mystical Protectors of the Cold
Creativity Unchained: Unlocking Your Wildest Ideas in 2025
Manifestation Mastery: 365 Days to Rewrite Your Reality
The Groundhog's Mirror: Reflecting on Change
The Weeping Angels' Christmas Curse
Burrowed in Time: A Groundhog Day Journey
Heartbeats: Poems to Share with Your Valentine
Dino Wicca: The Sacred Grimoire of Prehistoric Magick
Courage of the Pride: Finding Your Inner Roar
The Lion's Leap: Bold Moves for Big Results
Healthy Hustle: Achieving Without Overworking
Practical Manifesting: Turning Dreams into Reality in 2025
Jurassic Pharaohs: Unlocking the Magick of Ancient Egypt and Dino Wicca
The Happiness Equation: Small Changes for Big Joy
The Confidence Compass: Finding Your Inner Strength
Whispers in the Hollow: Tales of the Forgotten Beasts
Echoes from the Hollow: The Return of Forgotten Beasts
The Hollow Ascendant: The Rise of the Forgotten Beasts
The Relationship Reset: Building Better Connections
Mastering the Morning: How to Win the Day Before 8 AM
The Shadow's Dance: Groundhog Day Symbolism
Cupid's Kitchen: Quick Valentine's Day Recipes
Valentine's Day on a Budget: Love Without Breaking the Bank
Astrocraft: Aligning the Stars in the World of Minecraft
Forecasting Life: Groundhog Day Reflections
Bleeding Hearts: Twisted Tales of Valentine's Terror
Herbal Smoke Revolution: The Ultimate Guide to Nature's Cigarette Alternative
Winter's Wrath: The Complete Survival Blueprint for Extreme Freezes.

The Groundhog's Shadow: A Tale of Seasons
Burrowed Insights: Wisdom from the Groundhog
Sensual Strings: The Art of Erotic Bondage
Whispered Flames: Unlocking the Power of Fire Play
Forgotten Shadows: A Guide to Cryptids Lost to Time
Six Weeks of Secrets: Groundhog Day's Hidden Messages
Shadows and Cycles: Groundhog Day Reflections
The Art of Love Letters: Crafting the Perfect Message
Romantic Getaways at Home: Turning Your Space into Paradise
Purrfect Brews: A Cat Lover's Guide to Coffee and Companionship
The Groundhog's Wisdom: Timeless Lessons for Modern Life
The Shadow Oracle: Groundhog Day as a Predictor
Emerging from the Burrow: A Journey of Renewal
The Language of Love: Learning Your Partner's Love Style
Authorpreneur: The Ultimate Blueprint for Writing, Publishing, and Thriving as an Author
Weathering the Seasons: Groundhog Day Perspectives
Valentine's Day Magic: A Guide to Romantic Rituals
The Shadow Chronicles: Stories of Groundhog Day
Love and Laughter: Fun Games for Valentine's Day
AstroRealty: Unlocking the Stars for Property Success
The Groundhog's Path: A Guide to Seasonal Balance
Groundhog Day Diaries: Reflections in the Shadow
The Groundhog's Light: Illuminating the Path Ahead
Valentine's Traditions from Around the World
AI Wealth Revolution: Unlocking the Trillionaire Mindset
Love Rekindled: Reigniting Passion in Relationships
Single and Thriving: Self-Love on Valentine's Day
Emerald Legends: Mystical Tales of Ireland
Green Alchemy: Harnessing Nature's Magic
The Hearts of Horror: A Valentine's Day Nightmare

The Leprechaun's Guide to Wealth and Wisdom
Dancing with the Sidhe: Celebrating the Otherworld
Shamrocks and Shadows: Mysteries of the Green Isle
Emerald Energy: Harnessing Luck and Growth
The Gingerbread Golem's Valentine: A Sweetheart's Guide to Love and Enchantment
The Celtic Knot: Weaving Life and Destiny
Green Fire: Elemental Magic for St. Patrick's Day
Clover Chronicles: Finding Your Inner Luck
Ireland's Mystical Creatures: A Field Guide
Gingerbread Golem's Love Almanac
Prowl and Thrive: The Lion's Guide to Success
Love Alchemy: Transforming Your Life Through Heart Energy
WORLD DOMINATION: Woman's Rule 3:The New Life
The Midnight Rose: A Guide to Lunar Love Spells
The Forbidden Letters: Writing Your Own Love Prophecy
Luck and Lore: St. Patrick's Day for Modern Mystics
The Green Path: A Pagan Celebration of Renewal
The Dark Architect's Guide to Reprogramming Reality
Prankster's Paradise: A Guide to Harmless Hijinks
Manifest Your Reality: The Law of Attraction Simplified
The TARDIS Owner's Manual: Understanding the Doctor's Ship: *A complete guide to the TARDIS, its technology, secrets, and mysteries*
Starlit Romance: Astrology Secrets for Finding True Love
The Time Lord's Atlas: A Complete Guide to the Whoniverse: ***A breakdown of the locations, planets, and dimensions explored in Doctor Who***
Sweetheart Shadows: The Dark Side of Love and Attraction
February Fire: Reigniting Passion in Every Area of Life
The Self-Love Toolkit: 5 Ways to Embrace Who You Are
February Sparks: Ignite Your Dreams in 28 Days

March to Success: A 31-Day Action Blueprint
Ancient Paths: The 13 Sacred Principles of Dino Wicca
Echoes of Tomorrow: Navigating the AI Revolution
The Wellness Blueprint: Balancing Mind, Body, and Soul
Green Horizons: Sustainable Living for a Better Tomorrow
The AI Wealth Code: How to Make Millions with Automation
AI-Powered Creativity: Writing, Art, and Music for Profit
Extinction Rites: Rebirthing Your Soul Through Prehistoric Magick
Sacred Serpents tarot
Celestial Enchantment blank journal
Star Strains
Culinary Journeys: Exploring Global Flavors at Home
The Hollowvale Curse
The Hollowvale Harvest
The Egg of Transformation: Awakening Your Inner Power
Blooming Into Power: A Wiccan Guide to Spring Awakening
The Nightmare Nexus: The Third Doctor's Perilous Haunting
Digital Detox: Reclaiming Your Life in a Connected World
Ostara's Path: Walking the Spiral of Renewal
The Sacred Hare
Financial Freedom: Building Wealth in the Modern Age
Spring's Cauldron: Stirring the Waters of Change
The Hollowvale Pact
Quantum Consciousness: The Science of Reality Shifting
The Hollowvale Hunger
The Sacred Waters Within: A Witch's Guide to Hydrocephalus Magick
The Raven's Nest: Building a Life of Unshakable Stability
AI and the Human Mind: The Future of Intelligence
The Hollowvale Reckoning
Timeless Love: Building and Maintaining Lasting Relationships

The Raven's Roar: Unlocking Unstoppable Confidence
Raven Sight: Awakening Intuition and Inner Wisdom
The Butterfly Effect: Small Changes, Big Transformations
Taming the Boogeyman: How to Conquer Your Inner Fears
The Magick of Green: Awakening Earth's Energy in You
The Entrepreneurial Mindset: Secrets to Business Success
The Hollowvale End
The Shadow Luck Ritual: Reclaiming Power from Your Dark Side
Spring Magick for Beginners: A Simple Guide to Seasonal Energy Work
Doctor Who: The Hollowvale Conundrum
The March of Miracles: Unlocking Synchronicities in Spring
Unveiling the Cosmos: A Guide to Stargazing and Space Exploration
The Ultimate Guide to Surviving an Economic Collapse
The AI Gold Rush: How to Profit from the AI Revolution
Bastet's Shadow: The Hidden Power of Feline Magick
The Bastet Codex: Unlocking the Goddess's Magickal Secrets
Purring Spells: Harnessing Bastet's Healing Frequencies
Bastet's Nine Lives: Rebirth, Transformation, and Immortality Spells
Primal Currents: Hydrocephalus Magick in the Path of Dino Wicca
The Digital Gold Rush: Mastering E-Commerce and Online Sales
Future Shock: Adapting to the Next Decade of Change
The Quantum Mindset: Think Like a Billionaire
Sacred Motherhood: Awakening the Divine Feminine Within
The Mother's Spellbook: Enchantments for Love, Protection, and Prosperity
The Witch's Guide to Parenting: Raising Empowered and Intuitive Children

The Magick of Motherhood: Reclaiming Your Power Through Rituals

The Pagan Path to Self-Love: A Goddess's Guide to Worth and Confidence

Wild Woman Magick: Unleashing Your Primal Power

The Money Magnet Blueprint: Unlocking Unlimited Wealth

Biohacking 101: Unlock Your Body's Full Potential

The Wild Father: A Pagan Guide to Strength and Wisdom

The Sacred Masculine: Unlocking Your Inner Power

The Druid's Compass

The Warrior's Mindset

The Father's Fire

Odin's Path

Ancestral Bonds

The House That Whispers

The Magician's Code

The Wild Hunt

The Green Man's Path

The Altar of Success

The Shadow and the Sword

The High Priestess's Guide to Energy Healing

The Lunar Mother

The Sacred Self-Care Grimoire

The Womb Wisdom Codex

The Wheel of the Mother

The Witch's Guide to Manifestation

The Q2 Reset

The Ultimate Guide to AI-Powered Passive Income

Escape the 9-5

AI Feline Fortunes

The Tear-Stained Grimoire

Razorblade Runes

Cemetery Sirens

The Midnight Wristwatch
The Town That Forgets
AI Horror & Creepypasta
The Hollow Frequency
The Breach Echo
The Quiet Between Worlds
The Sigil of Tharan-Khul
Summon the Vault of Y'ha'ten
The Becoming Codex
The Profit of Az'ra-nar
The Drowned Logos
Echoes of the Eldritch Will
The Deep Ledger
Necronomicon of Networth
Covenant of the Wealthwyrm
The Whisperer's Manifesto
The Rites of Azh-K'luth
The Ark of the Crawling Coin
The Tithe of Shadows
Inkheart Abyss
The Timewinds of Y'ha-nthlei
The Spiral Labyrinth of Azag-Nirrh
The Gallifreyan Heresy of the Black Pharaoh
The Psalms of Nyog-Sotha
Black Rain Alchemy
The Infinite Maw
The Entropic Blueprint
The Oracle of Sh'guul
The Book of Breach
The Drowned Saint's Testament
Dreamcraft of the Sleeper God
The Silence Market
Cthonomics: The Dark Wealth Algorithm

Invocation of the Ten-Eyed King
Wealthbound to the Wyrm Below
Become the Unnameable
Codex of the Sovereign Flame
Rituals of Relentless Becoming
The Shadow Ascends
The Eyes Beneath You
The Will That Wakes Worlds
Silence Is a Weapon
The Mirror That Screams
The Whisper Between Moments
The Mind That Devours Fear
The Myth of the Finished Self
The Architect of Your Madness
The Voice You've Buried
The Discipline of Madness
Stormborn: Awakening Your Inner Tempest
The Mind That Ate Time
Unbind Your Becoming
The Pact You Owe Yourself
The Devourer's Diet
The Acid That Carves the Path
The Tower You Must Burn
The Breath Between Worlds
Speak Like the Deep
The Labyrinth Within
The Spine of the Sea God
Rejection Is a Portal
The Crown You Refused
The Scar Is the Spell
The Lightless Flame
The Habit of Becoming Horrific
ChickenJockey Chaos

The Gatekeeper Within
You Are Not Your Name
The Compass of the Mad
The Archive of Unsent Letters
What the Mirror Can't Show You
The Knife You Needed
Worship Nothing, Become Everything
The Other Voice
The Body the World Forgot
The Vein of the Void
The Black Bone Codex
The Puzzle of the Hidden Self (Millennium Puzzle)
The Eye That Sees the Lie *(Millennium Eye)*
The Ring of Return (Millennium Ring)
The Rod of Relentless Will *(Millennium Rod)*
The Tally of the Soul (Millennium Tauk/Necklace)
The Key to the Locked Timeline (Millennium Key)
The Scale of Sacred Decisions (Millennium Scales)
Inferno Bites: The UnOfficial Minecraft Lava Cookbook
Rot in the Attic
Prana: The Hidden Force of Your Infinite Self
The Shadow Realm Within: Transforming Darkness Into Destiny
The Borderland Collapse
Claws of Protection: Bastet's Defensive Magick
Mr. Ring-a-Ding's Madness
Yugioh Astrology: Celestial Deckcraft and Duel Destiny (2026–2027 Edition)
The Seal You Signed: Unlocking the Power You Once Feared
The Puzzle of Infinite Minds: Unlocking the Mentalism Hidden Within
The Eye That Mirrors the All: Secrets of Inner Reflection
Doctor Who: The Toymaker's Broadcast

The Rod of Eternal Flow: Commanding the Currents of Vibration

Golden Eyes of Bastet: Enhancing Psychic Vision

The Key of Dual Forces: Balance Within the Polarity

The Scales of Living Rhythm: Timing the Dance of Life

The Necklace of Hidden Cause: Weaving the Webs of Fate

The Ring of Secret Masters: Rising Through the All Within All

Daggers of the Dying Deep

Bastet's Wealth and Fortune Magick: Prosperity Rituals of the Goddess

The Tide that Speaks

The Scrolls of Petosiris: 13 Rituals from the Feathered Eye

Petosiris and the Living Plague of Osirion

Feline Fire: Bastet's Passion and Love Magick

The Star Altar of Petosiris

Bastet's Whiskers: Supernatural Sensory Magick

The Bastet Grimoire

Feeding the Shadows

The Mouthless Prayer

The Spiral Wound

Becoming the Ibis: Lessons from Petosiris's Mind

The Crimson Coven: Cola Magick for Sweet Dominion

Sacred Cat's Paw

The Soda Zodiac: A Flavor for Every Sign

Covenant of the Crawling Flame

The Ink of Ish'Zur

Frothroot: The Thirst That Ate the World

The Golden Glyphs of Prosperity

The Etherbind Codex

Echoes of the Resistance: Reclaiming the You That Survived

Harnessed Minds: Breaking Free from Mental Control

The Eyes in the Smoke

Rootwake: The Carbon Covenant
Skitter Logic: Unlearning the Fear That Built You
Doctor Who: The World That Froths
Rootwake: The Fizz That Rewrites Flesh
Rootwake: Frothfather of the World
The Holly Pact: Blood Beneath the Mistletoe
The 2nd Mass Principle: Building Unbreakable Tribes
Web of Wits: A Survival Guide to Encounters with Anasi the Spider (Aunt Nancy)
The Hexbreaking Handbook: Effective Spells to Remove Curses
Pop Alchemy: Transform Your Life One Sip at a Time
The Mason Code: Leading in Unleadable Times
Petosiris and the Fifth Chamber of Thoth
The Ether Seed Within
The Parent of Tomorrow
Petosiris's Pyramid of Perpetual Wealth
Unlearn the World
Grimoire of the Hollow Tongue
Zodiac Weeds: Finding Your Strain Through the Stars
Aquarius Rises in the Bank
The Sugar God's Smile
The Skinclock Reversal: Biohacking the Face of Time
Debtburn: How to Obliterate What You Owe Forever
The Ice Cream Oracle: What Your Cone Says About Your Future
Silence Is Sovereignty: The Power of Being Unreadable
The Wind That Whispers Through Stone
Path of the Four Directions
Doctor Who: The Maestro's Symphony of Endings
Oxygen Grail: Breathing to Undo the Clock
Zodiacal Collapse: When Stars Devour Time
Teachings from the Red Sand Silence

Doctor Who: Omega – The Broken Equation
Memory Wipe Your Past: Start Over Like a MiB
Mitochondria Prime: Ignite the Core of Youth
A Nest of Roaches
Grub from the Galaxy: MiB Recipes You'll Never Forget
Whiskers of Power: Bastet's Guide to Inner Sovereignty
The Gift Must Cost Them: Negotiation Through Unequal Exchange
The Worm Guys' Wealth Code: Hustle Like an Alien
Bug Out: The Edgar Method for Ruthless Goal Setting
Weaving Life with Spiderwoman's Pattern
Doctor Who: The Rani's Renaissance
How to Get a Job (If You're a Puppygirl)
Speak Through Others: The Art of Proxy Power
T-Rex Your Trauma: Reclaim the Power of Your Primal Self
The Black Briefcase: How MiB Stay Wealthy in Silence
The Thirst Beyond Reason: Understanding Diabetes Insipidus From the Inside Out
Backwoods Witchcraft for Billionaires: The Pagan Path from Dirt Roads to Gold Roads
The Moonshine Grimoire: Fermented Spells for Abundance
The Nameless Geometry
The Wraith's Mixtape: Spellcasting with Songs of Sorrow
The Gallifreyan Gentleman: Silent Wealth, Sonic Confidence, and the Doctor's Code of Living
Sugar Water Confidence
Dino Totems: Spirit Guides from Earth's First Gods
Pumpkin Sigils & Ritual Smoke
The Hózhó Compass
The Distortus Discipline – Order from Inner Mutation
Witchcraft for the Cold-Blooded Soul
Moonlight Over the Blessingway
Water, Interrupted: When the Body Forgets How to Hold On

Deformed but Divine: Embracing Your Asymmetry
Hexes in the Henhouse: The Farm Witch's Guide to Power
The Reversed Flame: A Grimoire of Inverted Power
Salt, Cells, and Sanity: Reclaiming Balance with Diabetes Insipidus
King of the Broken: Crowning the Flawed Self
Moonlight Scars: Emo Moon Magick and the Art of Lunar Sorrow
Noose Spells: Magick of the Hanging Rope
The Goth Cathedral: Rituals of the Broken and Beautiful
The Cretaceous Codex: Dino Spirits and Fossil Magick
The Turkey Bones Ritual
Nine Lives of Manifestation: Unlocking Bastet's Reality Codes
Chaos Muscles: Building Strength from Twisted Pain
Emo Blood Magick: The Veins of Power
The 3AM Flood: Nighttime Urination, Sleep Loss, and the DI Spiral
The Silence Between the Stars
The Lemon Method: Sour Your Way to Success
Starlit Sovereign
The Rite of Twelve Gates: Walking the Gates of the Duat.
Cornbread and Conjure: Recipes for Riches and Rootwork
The Black Rose Rituals: Emo Love Spells and Obsession Magick
The Eternal Goodbye: Death Magick and Rebirth Rituals
Sinkrot: The Drain That Remembers
The Hybrid Mindset: Thinking Beyond Evolution
Bone Dry: Navigating Dehydration Before It Breaks You
Wreathcraft: Winter Sigils and Yuletide Spells
The Rite of Twelve Mouths
S'mores of the Damned: Haunted Recipes for Halloween Night

Rethink the Drink: A Beverage Survival Guide for DI Warriors

The Shadow Chord: Guitar Magick and Sonic

Malformed Yet Majestic: Leading When You Feel Wrong Inside

The Cursed Diary: Ink-Stained Spells of the Emo Soul

Anxiety Off Switch: Emergency Reset for a Fried Nervous System

The Energy Heist: How to Take Back Your Life from Drainers

Beyond the Bathroom: Rebuilding Your Social Life With DI

Coyote's Gift for Decision Makers

Ghoul-Goo: Spooky S'mores You'll Die For

Echoes in the Mirror: Scrying and Self-Destruction Magick

Thread and Thorn: Stitching Spells from Rural Cloth

The Mogwai Mind: Building Untouchable Wealth from Small Ideas

Be Your Own Guide: Trust Your Inner Compass

Hormones in Chaos: The Endocrine Puzzle of Diabetes Insipidus

ChronoCleanse: Detox Your Biological Timeline

The Limb You Hide Is the One That Saves You

Leaves, Bones, and Whisper Spells

The Dinosaur Mindset: Prehistoric Tactics for Modern Wealth

Clawing Back Control: A Bastet Method for Boundaries and Empowerment

Samhain Codes of the Forgotten

Orange Alchemy: The Autumnal Spellbook

Monster Within, Master Without

The Sigil That Sleeps

Hearthcraft: Yule Hearth Sigils and Winter Warmth Spells

Temple of the Purring Moon: Rituals from Bastet's Lineage

When the Earth Remembers Your Footsteps

Food for Mood: Eat to Heal Depression, Not Just Survive It
Witch of the Kudzu Vine: Southern Pagan Wealth Secrets
The Invisible Diagnosis: Advocating for Yourself With DI
The Coffin's Lullaby: Sleep Magick and Nightmares as Portals
Ashes of the Will: Rituals for Erasing the Self
The Fracture Rite: Shattering the Magickal Core
Funeral Candles: The Art of Emo Flame Magick
The Black Grimoire: A Blank Ritual for Writing in Absence
Phantom Thirst: A Halloween Survival Guide for Diabetes Insipidus
The Hollow Crown: Emo Royalty and Magick of the Outcast King
Sandpainting for the Soul
Falling Into Balance: Using the Extra Hour to Recalibrate Life
100 Southern Superstitions That Still Work
The DI Child: A Parent's Guide to Raising Hydrated, Happy Kids
The Jungle of Shame: Escaping the Hidden Lab of Doubt
The Witch's Toast: S'mores Spells and Creepy Confections
The Hoodoo Pantry: Spells from the Mason Jar
The Immortal Fortune: Secret Wealth Lessons from Captain Jack Harkness
The Specter's Embrace: Magick for Channeling Ghostly Lovers
Grateful Waters: A Thanksgiving Survival Guide for Diabetes Insipidus
The Seizure Gospel
Harvestbind: Autumn Sigils and Samhain Spells
Doctor Who: The Algorithmic Awakening
Silent Nights, Steady Waters: A Christmas Survival Guide for Diabetes Insipidus
The Extra Hour Effect: How One Hour Can Transform Everything

Blade Between the Breaths

Running with the Mountain Shadows

Echoes of the Failed Experiment – Becoming a Living Legacy

Swamp Witches & River Ghosts: Real Southern Hauntings

Cornbread Prophecies: Magical Recipes from a Southern Table

Doctor Who: The Signal in the Star

Bloomcraft: Spring Sigils and Equinox Enchantments

Vanisher: How to Disappear from the Internet Without Losing Your Life

The Ultimate Christmas Cookie Cookbook

The Unbreakable Parent: How to Mentally Survive Raising Kids in a Broken World

Time Debt: How to Reclaim the Hours You Didn't Know You Lost

One Month, One Million: Unconventional Cash Creation Tactics

Doctor Who: The Cyber Conversion Protocol

Black Friday Frenzy: The Art of Finding Hidden Online Deals

The Grimoire Buried Under the Apple Tree

Digital Couponing Masterclass: Your Step-by-Step Guide to Black Friday Savings

The Fire Inside the Flint

Shadows on the Ceiling: The Emo Guide to Astral Magick

The Bone-Eaters Beneath Us

Black Friday Bundle Blueprint: Creating Irresistible Product Packages for Maximum Sales

Thirteen Nights of Unbinding

Doctor Who: Engines of Influence

Pumpkin Spice Alchemy: Recipes of Fire and Frost

When Raptor Met Rexy: Prehistoric Lessons in Wild Romance

Oblivion's Candle: Burn the Path Behind You

Campfire Curses and Chocolate: A Halloween S'mores Grimoire

The Wallet That Wasn't Mine: Breaking Free from Inherited Scarcity

The Cola Zodiac: What Your Fizz Says About Your Fate

Frostfire Fortune: Unlocking Winter's Hidden Prosperity

Signal Jamming: Detox Your Brain from Info Overload

The Dust of the Forgotten Rite

The Golden Cat Sigils: Drawing Power in Bastet's Name

Mud Magick: The Prosperity of Getting Dirty

Savory Spicefall: Beyond the Pumpkin Pie

Pumpkin Spice Apothecary Kitchen

The Pumpkin Spice Economy: Turning Trends into Billions

The Ember Veil: 13 Nights of Fire Magick

Financial Freeze: When Earning Triggers Panic

The Gingerbread Alchemist: Sweet Recipes with a Twist

Biosynth Power: Programming Yourself from Scratch

Echoes from the Talking Circle

Truffle Alchemy: Fungus of Fortune

Spores of Power: The Truffle Witch's Handbook

Doctor Who: The Tower That Speaks

The Mycelium Veil: Truffle Magick Unbound

Broke But Ashamed: Healing the Shame Wound of Debt

The Evergreen Mind: Growth Through Winter Stillness

The Black Veil Truffle Rite

The Voice Beneath Symbols

Witchlight on the Bayou: Swamp Spells for Sovereignty

I Grew Up Poor and Now I Sabotage My Success

The Lantern of Hollow Souls

Shutdown Survival: A Citizen's Guide to Thriving When Government Stops

When Abundance Feels Like a Threat: Healing the Hidden Fears of Enough

The Scarecrow Grimoire
Owls of the October Veil
Candlewax and Curses: A Halloween Spellbook
Excavating the Inner Fossil – Transforming Fossilized Thoughtforms into Tools of Power
The Yule Witch's Spellbook: Magick for the Holiday Season
Haunted Christmas: Ghost Stories for Winter Nights
The Christmas Survival Guide: Thriving Through the Chaos
The Bone Orchard Rites
Haunted Commerce: The Ghost in the Marketplace
When Money Triggers the Inner Child
Silent Night with the Silence: A Christmas Thriller
The Lightning Crown: Living and Leading Through Seizures
TARDIS Tidings: Festive Stories from the Whoniverse
Autumn Reset: Slowing Down Without Falling Behind
The Trillion Dollar Soul: Rewriting the Currency of Reality
Truffle Eclipse Magick
Micro-Manifestations: Quick Magick That Works
5-Minute Rituals for Busy Witches
The Marshmallow Massacre: Halloween Treats with a Sinister Twist
Blood and Blackberry Thorns
Magickal Mornings: Rituals for a Blessed Christmas Day
Embers of the All-Hallows Fire
The Pumpkin Market Collapse
The Hour You Gained: Transforming Time Into Power
The Chamber Must Be Sealed: Mastering the Power of Controlled Access
The Cursed Manuscript of Petosiris
The Festive Hearth: Creating Holiday Traditions
Darkness Rising: Thriving as Nights Grow Longer
Harvesting Time: Turning the Year's End Into Your New Beginning

Petosiris and the 13th Zodiac Key

Wagewound: When Paychecks Become Identity Prisons

Walls That Watch

The Silent Feast: Rituals of Power in the Longest Night

The Distortus Legacy : Becoming a Deformed King in a Perfect World

The Hollow Masks

The Gratitude Furnace: Forging Gold from Thanks

Feast of Inner Gold: Eating for Energy and Enlightenment

Haunted Commerce: The Season of Spending Spirits

Fear Bonds: How Panic Creates Profit

Black Friday E-Commerce Playbook: Sales Tactics to Skyrocket Your Holiday Revenue

Budgeting for Black Friday: A Holiday Savings Planner

Haunting the Harvest Moon

The Warrior's Water: Emergency Preparedness for People With DI

The First Sip of the Year: A New Year's Survival Guide for Diabetes Insipidus

Doctor Who: The Thirteenth Node

The Unseen Struggle: Mental Health, Anxiety, and Chronic Thirst

The Hearth's Hidden Ledger: Counting Energies as Currency

The Gift Alchemist: Turning Any Offering Into Gold

The Papyrus of the Bound Spirit

The Magick of Leftovers: Transmutation in the Fridge

Frost and Fortune: Christmas Wealthcraft for the Modern Magus

Last-Minute Gifts: Creative Ideas on a Budget

10 Secrets to Surviving Holiday Crowds

The Witch's Dow Jones

The Witches' Graveyard Shift

Pumpkin Sigils: Carving Rites for Midnight Power

The Secret Shopper's Black Friday Guide: How to Get Early Access and VIP Deals

Fever in the Foundation

The Neuralyzer Reset: Reprogram Your Morning Routine

Lightning Lessons of the White Painted Woman

The Enchanted Snowflake

The Magic Sip: Surviving Disney Parks with Diabetes Insipidus

The One Who Draws Through You

Santa's Secrets: A Magical Holiday Planner

Silent Bells, Loud Miracles: Self-Help for the Season of Stillness

The Sugar Spell Codex: Confectionary Magick of Christmas

Autumn Hexcraft: Fallen Leaves, Fallen Barriers

Sleep Like a Fortress: Build a Life Where Insomnia Can't Survive

Nowhere Was Ever Home

Christmas Under the Stars: A Celestial Holiday Guide

Rentproof: How to Never Be Evicted Again

Workless: Escape the 9-5 Without Being Broke

The Gilded Gift: A Wealth Altar for Christmas Morning

The Black Friday Grimoire

The Hollowing: Ceremonies of Spiritual Collapse

Doctor Who: The Nameless Signal

Where the Eagle Hides His Courage

The Dwarf Tyrant's Ascent: Claiming Power in a World of Giants

The Currency of the Dead: Trading with Spectral Bankers

The Icebound Witch: Survival and Magick in the Cold

The Emergency Money Mind: Constant Crisis, Zero Calm

Thirst & Roses: A Valentine's Survival Guide for Diabetes Insipidus

Springing Into Clarity: Mastering the Energy Shift of Daylight Saving

Speed of the Nanotyrant: Agile Strategies for Life's Hunt

The 90-Day Reset: A Science-Backed Guide to Reinvent Yourself Before the New Year

The Coil of Thorns

Timegates Unleashed

Dopamine Fasting 2.0: Rewiring Your Brain in a World of Overstimulation

The Nanotyrannus Mutation: Embracing Your Differentiated Form

Unwritten January: How to Use the Blank Page of the Year to Re-Author Your Life

Feast of the Forgotten Spirits: Ancestor Magick for the Holidays

The Burnout Codex: A System for Thriving Beyond Stress

I Don't Deserve to Have Money

When the King Doesn't See You: The Shadow Predator's Guide

The Reset Ritual :A Guide to Shedding Last Year's Weight—Emotional and Physical—by Spring Cleaning Your Soul

Calendar Alchemy: Learn to Bend Time and Productivity around Your Natural Rhythms

The Mirror Contract: A One-Sentence Agreement with Yourself that Unlocks Real Change

The Nile Formula: Sacred Flow for Millionaire Minds

Forward Momentum: Productivity Rituals for the Lost Hour

Harvest Gold: Wealth Magick of Pumpkin Spice Commerce

The Magick of Christmas Lights: Illuminating Holiday Rituals

Cranberry Crown: Royal Self-Worth through Ritual Meals

Petosiris and the Worms of the Feathered Throne

The Evergreen Equation: Self-Help for Sustained Growth

The Rain Will Wash Us Away: Emo Weather Magick

Snowlight Shadows: Magick Under Frozen Stars

Doctor Who: Merger of Empires

The Light Within the Feast: Magickal Wealth of Yuletide Flame

Momentum Machines: Small Habits Designed to Snowball into Unstoppable Forward Motion

Calm Spells: Magickal Solutions for Anxiety Relief

Santa's Final List: The Naughty Never Leave

The Mystic's Guide to Banishing Worry

The Silence Dividend: Turning Quiet Mornings into Compounding Growth All Year

Charmed Stillness: Rituals to Ease the Mind

Blood Spiral Ascension

The Vanishing Heart Invocation

Crystal Calm: Harnessing Stones for Anxiety

The Nano Tyrant Code: Strength in the Small Predator

The Energy Ledger: Accounting Methods for Vitality, Not Just Money

Snowglobe Mindset: Shake Up Your Thoughts, Settle Into Peace

The Weight of the Feather: Anubis's Codes for Soul Balance

Pocket Peppermint Power: Tiny Rituals for Big Holiday Energy

Shadowkeeper of the Golden Jackal: Anubis's Path to Energetic Protection

The Witch's Breath: Anxiety Relief Through Magickal Breathing

The Tiny Ember: Pocket Motivation for Cold Days

Stocking Sorcery: Mini Spells for Holiday Luck and Prosperity

Warm Hands, Steady Heart: Micro Grounding for Winter Anxiety

The Fourteenth Doctor: A New Beginning (David Tennant, 2022–2023)

The Fifteenth Doctor: Rewriting the Stars
(Ncuti Gatwa, 2023–2025)

Santa's Shortcut to Success: Micro Habits for a Better New Year

The Midnight Cocoa Manifesto: Comfort Rituals for Hard Nights

Why I Can't Save: Trauma Blocks to Financial Planning

Dino Brain, Mega Goals: Rewire Yourself for Savage Success.

Jurassic Profit: Unearth Your Inner Millionaire Fossil

Scales & Softness: Dating with Dino Heart

Carnotaurus Dreams.

Red Willow Thinking.

Reindeer Resilience: How to Keep Going When You're Exhausted

Candlewick Courage: Lighting Strength in Dark Seasons.

Elf-Mode Focus: Fast Attention Fixes for Busy Seasons

Futureproof Feelings: Emotional Skill-Building for Resilience No Matter What the New Year Brings

The 90-Day Rewire: Transform Your Neural Pathways Before Spring Blooms

Jolly Rich: Christmas Micro-Money Magick for Fast Prosperity.

Gingerbread Gratitude: Mini Practices for a Happier Holiday

Get Some Tarot cards: https://www.makeplayingcards.com/sell/apophis-occult-shop

Get some shirts: https://www.bonfire.com/store/apophis-shirt-emporium/

Instagrams:
@apophis_enterprises,
@apophisbookemporium,
@apophisscardshop
Twitter: @apophisenterpr1
Tiktok:@apophisenterprise
Youtube: @sg1fan23477
Hive: @sg1fan23477
CheeLee: @SG1fan23477

Podcast: Apophis Chat Zone: https://open.spotify.com/show/5zXbrCLEV2xzCp8ybrfHsk?si=fb4d4fdbdce44dec

Newsletter: https://apophiss-newsletter-27c897.beehiiv.com/

If you want to support me or see posts of other projects that I have come over to: **buymeacoffee.com/mpetchinskg**

I post there daily several times a day

Get your Dinowicca or Christmas themed digital products, especially Santa Raptor songs and other musics. Here: **https://sg1fan23477.gumroad.com**

Apophis Yuletide Digital has not only digital Christmas items, but it will have all things with Dinowicca as well as other Digital products.

www.ingramcontent.com/pod-product-compliance
Lightning Source LLC
LaVergne TN
LVHW022228200926
848481LV00006B/2170
* 9 7 9 8 2 9 5 4 5 6 4 6 6 *